SARAH PALIN

FAITH
FAMILY
COUNTRY

Susan Sherwood Parr

Bridge-Logos
Alachua, Florida 32615

Bridge-Logos

Alachua, FL 32615 USA

Sarah Palin: Faith, Family, Country
by Susan Sherwood Parr

Copyright ©2008 by Bridge-Logos

Printed in the United States of America.

Library of Congress Catalog Card Number: 2008938419
International Standard Book Number 978-0-88270-861-4

Material in chapter 6: Copyright © 2008, The Speakout Foundation and OnTheIssues.org, Jesse Gordon, editor-in-chief. Used by permission.

Cover photo: © 2008 Judy Patrick /AlaskaStock.com

Cover design and layout by Elizabeth Nason

Childhood photos of Sarah Palin used by permission of the Heath family.

G352.316.N.m809.35240

DEDICATION

To my dear husband, author Monte R. Parr

Acknowledgements

Thanks and appreciation for those who
graciously helped on this project …

To my media consultant, Lindsey Boatman

To my son Chris Livingston

For the kind help from Sarah's family and friends:
Sally Heath
Chuck Heath
Mary Ellan Moe
Ruth Andree
Deanna Andree
Heyde Hackel
Karena Forster
Ben Harrell

Special thanks to Lloyd and Peggy Hildebrand,
Steve Becker, Elizabeth Nason, and the
Bridge-Logos team who brought it all together

Contents

Everybody's Talking About Sarah

Ben Harrell owns the Mocha Moose, a coffee shop in Wasilla. Karena Forster is Harrell's daughter. She shares this story about Sarah:

I have been serving Sarah coffee for many years. I remember her coming through in the morning on her way to drop kids off at school.

She would come in with her hair in a ponytail or half bun and no make up on, sometimes still in jammy pants and a t-shirt.

I remember one of the other baristas had seen her one morning coming through for her usual skinny white chocolate mocha. She took Sarah's order, shut her window, and made a sigh. I asked her what was the matter. Her reply was, "I was hoping that her beauty was all makeup, but it's not! She is just as gorgeous with no makeup. She has flawless skin."

I still remember that day. Sarah is a beautiful woman and seeing her in the morning with no makeup on and in her jammies just makes her a real down-to-earth person.

One time, she and her husband, Todd, came through the drive-thru at the Mocha Moose, with the Suburban full of kids. They were on their way out to their cabin to spend the New Year's holiday. They were all dressed up and looked sharp. I told them I wanted to "hang with the governor." They just laughed and we sat there having small talk. It was neat.

Another time my father heard that she was in town. This was just after Sarah's son Trig was born. He hurried and gathered a cute stuffed moose, some coffee, candy, and some other gift items and wrote Sarah and newborn Trig a note. He sent it down to the drive-thru for her. That morning when she arrived at the drive-thru for her coffee, the girls gave the gifts to her. She was really happy. Later my dad received a thank you card and birth announcement of Trig. He was so proud of that card and was just giddy with excitement. He hung it up on his bulletin board at the coffee house.

★ ★ ★

"I believe John McCain to be an honorable man of integrity. Sarah Palin seems to be exactly who he told us she was. She has as much experience (maybe more) than Clinton when he came to the White House.

"Sarah Palin appears to be down to earth and one of us 'common' folks who struggle with balancing family, work, and financial obligations. I am delighted to see a woman of character and experience being chosen by McCain. I particularly like that she is a Christian woman of prayer and faith but doesn't appear to hit people over the head with it."

Chaplain (Lieutenant Colonel USAR) Ronald H. Leggett
Walter Reed Army Medical Center

★ ★ ★

"The nation is well served when people with strong values accept the mantle of leadership. Sarah Palin is such a person.

"I am deeply gratified to see the personal and political integrity of someone like Sarah Palin dedicating her life to public service."

Congressman Steve Pearce
Founding Member Congressional Prayer Caucus

★ ★ ★

"'For such a time as this....' That's what the Bible says about another female leader [Queen Esther—Esther 4:14, NKJV] who burst on the national scene and dramatically altered history.

"Sarah Palin's story just may have elements of this famous event. But we do know that God directs the promotion of kings and leaders and His hand is certainly on the political chessboard once again. Sarah Palin's rise to national prominence has been met by a level of venom not seen since the days of Clarence Thomas, but for a woman who can brave the Alaska wilderness, the wimps at 'Saturday Night Live' don't seem much of a threat.

"Whatever happens, in the November 2008 election, Sarah Palin will not be changed, she will remain a woman of God, a patriot, a mother, wife and leader. You can almost hear the ceiling shatter."

Chip Lusko
Pastor, Calvary of Albuquerque
Co-producer Epicenter Documentary
General Manager Connection Communications

★ ★ ★

"The 2008 Republican nomination of Sarah Palin for Vice President of the United States has certainly been making waves across the country, and rightly so. Sarah Palin has distinguished herself as a servant to the people —not a self-serving, power hungry, Washington elitist.

"Sarah Palin is a woman of integrity, holding to conservative values and is a shining example of someone who truly represents the people she was called to serve. Her promises to rid the government of bureaucracy, government waste, and corruption is not wishful thinking, but rather the words of a woman who has been sent to us on a mission to make our nation once again, a beacon of freedom, prosperity and peace in the world. I believe Sarah Palin to be a true patriot who, if elected, along with the next president of the United States will fulfill her destiny as one of our nations great leaders."

George J. Arnold, National Director
Impact for Life Ministries, Inc.

★ ★ ★

"Sarah Palin appeals to the hard-working women, because she has accomplished incredible success and struggled as a wife and the mother of five beautiful children, and she has become a respectable role model worthy of a following.

"The women who banner the Sarah Palin platform have never had a woman stand up for them with her moxie, ideology, integrity, and honesty. These women do not champion the leftist political atmosphere because they are successful hard-working contributors and are brutally taxed because of their success.

"Brilliantly hand picked by John McCain during the 2008 Republican National Convention, Sarah Palin was strategically an ideal Republican vice-presidential candidate choice. She was quickly, once again, put into a spotlight. John McCain was humble enough to stand aside as Palin got the majority of the media attention for a while. McCain is basking in the wise choice he made in selecting Palin as a running mate."

Monte R. Parr, Author
Board Member, Life to the World Ministries, Inc.

★ ★ ★

"From a college-age perspective, Sarah Palin represents what an honest and influential person ought to be. I feel she carries herself with noble grace, without a need for typical, shifty-eyed politicking.

"American political leaders are supposed to remain single-minded under heavy burdens. Politics is a complex cosmos of endless lobbying on all sides. Politicians, at times, must face misguided and corrupt court rulings, heart-heavy, special-interest groups, and people with their own agendas.

"We need Sarah Palin to break the mold and set an example in Washington. She can do it—of this I'm confident. Sarah is single-minded, guileless, and sincere. She is brilliant both in speech and in action, and is determined and powerfully motivated. Sarah has proven herself to be pure-hearted, headstrong, and wise. I think our Founding Fathers would be proud of Sarah Palin.

"We have hit a homerun. We've been given a gift. I pray for more enlightened leaders to come."

Christopher J. Livingston
New Mexico Delegation, 2008 Republican National Convention
Representative to the Pentagon for Books for the Troops

★ ★ ★

"As Kierkegaard reminds us, 'A possibility is a hint from God. One must follow it.' The nomination of Sarah Palin, a leader with heart, soul, and intellect, wielded for the common good, heralds the possibility of an essential era, one of moral integrity, achievement of values, and reason, which is essential for the restoration of this, our America the beautiful."

H. Raven Rose
Author, Screenwriter
"Star Speaker" Screenwriting Expo, 2004, 2006

CHAPTER 1

Sarah's Early Years

Sarah Louise Heath Palin was born February 11, 1964, in Sandpoint, Idaho. She is the third of four children born to Charles R. and Sarah Heath. The family moved to Alaska when Sarah was two months old. Her older brother, Chuck Jr., was two years old, her sister Heather had just turned one, and the youngest sister, Molly, was soon to be born.

The Heath men did everything from running trap lines to putting out crab pots, and hunting goats and seals. They had their own private excavations of the remnants from the Klondike Gold Rush.

In 1969, the family settled in the small town

of Wasilla, Alaska. They worked hard as a family, doing what it took to make a living. They grew up unafraid and looked forward to every adventure. They grew up with the great outdoors as their playground. They ran, hiked, hunted, and fished. The family was athletic and regularly ran 5k and 10k races. They did what kids do who don't play a lot of video games or watch hours of television.

The Heath home faced the Talkeetna Mountains. The mountain range helps form the Matanuska and Susitna Valleys and is surrounded by towns such as Wasilla, Palmer, Sutton, and Talkeetna.

Those mountains are also home to Hatcher Pass, a popular ski and snowboarding area in winter, and hiking and berry-picking area in summer. Independence Mine, another historical site, is also located in Hatcher Pass.

Most of the land is state-owned and is home to many large mammals including grizzly, brown, and black bear, moose, caribou, wolves, wolverine, and Dall sheep.

Sarah grew up hunting, fishing, skiiing, and enjoying the natural beauty of the great Alaskan wilderness.

CHAPTER 2

Sarah Barracuda

Sally Heath's faith in God imparted inspiration and strength to her children. Sally is still deeply involved in the lives of her children, supporting them with their needs as parents, and just being a great grandparent.

A former teacher, Chuck Heath, is quite an achiever. The Heath home holds trophies of his many

adventures. The knowledge and experience he's gained in life he shares. Since his retirement from teaching school, that knowledge and experience is now with the U.S. Department of Agriculture's Wildlife Services Program. Chuck's spirit of adventure and vast knowledge of science and the outdoors has been a source of inspiration for many years to his students, his own children, and every life he touches.

Young Sarah attended Wasilla High School. She was a leader even at that young age and headed up the Fellowship of Christian Athletes chapter at her school. She was also point guard and captain of the school's basketball team. Her team won the Alaska small-school basketball championship in 1982. She hit a critical free throw in the last seconds of the game, even though she was suffering from a stress fracture in her ankle. Because of that intense play, she was nicknamed "Sarah Barracuda."

Jerry Russell remembers the seventh-grader Sarah as a quiet girl, a good student in his social studies class, and a fierce competitor on the hardwood. Jerry coached Sarah and the Wasilla seventh-grade girls' basketball team in 1977. Carol, his wife, was the high school registrar and secretary.

The Russells, both outdoor sports enthusiasts, moved to Alaska in 1966 for adventure and the state's excellent teacher employment benefits. They returned to Arkansas in 1986. Jerry, 67, spent his childhood years in Wiseman. He and Carol, 66, met in college at Beebe.

During an interview at the Russell home, Carol produced a series of Wasilla Junior High School Memories books showing school-days pictures of the

Sarah Heath (Palin), No. 22, was the point guard of the Wasilla Warriors in 1982 when they won the state championship.

young Sarah Heath with big teeth, dark hair, and the eyeglasses with heavy frames that she wore on the basketball court.

"Oh, yes. She was a good player," Jerry said. "There was just no 'quit' in her."

A now-famous photograph of Sarah Heath fighting for a basketball on the gym floor during a Wasilla High School basketball game accurately depicts the attitude the basketball standout brought to the game. "That tenacious spirit was no doubt a character trait that brought Palin to confront corrupt Alaska politicians and later to the floor of the GOP National Convention

Heather, Chuck, and Sarah Heath.

as Sen. John McCain's pick for the vice presidential side of the GOP ticket," Jerry said.

The game was with rival Palmer Public Schools, 11 miles from Wasilla schools. The game had come down to the last seconds and Wasilla was two points down when Russell called a time-out.

"Sarah was our best shooter so we wanted to get the ball to her and we did, and the other team just covered her up," Russell said. "I don't know how she got the shot off, but she did and it missed.

"The game ended and she got on the bench and buried her face in her hands crying.

"I went and put my arm around her and said: 'Come on now. It's OK. It's just a game.'"

"She said, 'I know, but we lost."

Russell said he was involved with thousands of students during his career in teaching and school administration. He remembers the problem students the most, but the four children of Chuck and Sally Heath were memorable, too, for their successes in the classroom and in athletics.

"I doubt I could count 20 kids I can remember," said Chuck, "but I remember all of the Heath kids."

In another game, Russell recalls that Sarah, at point guard, wasn't listening to the coach's instructions.

"My rule was that if a player had to be taken out of the game they would sit by me until I could explain why they were taken out.

"I asked her: 'Why weren't you listening to me?'

"She said: 'Coach Russell, you told us if we ever saw a chance to score to take it. I was doing what you told me to do, so put me back in.'"

Russell said he was amused almost to laughter by the outburst. "I had to turn away from her."

This same commitment is obvious in every endeavor undertaken by Sarah Palin.

Heyde Hackel is a teacher for children with special needs. She was a member of the Wasilla High School 1982 State-championship girls' basketball team. She has known Sarah Palin for many years; they both attended the same elementary school.

Heyde has many significant memories of Sarah Palin. They were in the same junior high school band. Sarah played the flute, and Heyde played the clarinet. They also played volleyball together, and then they joined the girls's basketball team. Hackel says, "We did a lot of things together."

Heyde said that Sarah was particularly good at rebounding, shooting from outside, and three-pointers. She said, "What she didn't get in points, she made up for in assists."

The high school yearbook reveals that Sarah was a member of the honor society, and she was the treasurer of the Student Council. That same yearbook provides us with an insight into the depth of Sarah's spirituality, for this quote was attributed to her: "He is the Light, and in the Light there is Life."

Heyde remembers Sarah as a genuine, very popular person who was always kind to everyone.

Chapter 3

The Greatest Influence

S arah credits her upbringing for her strong faith.

"Whether or not I was an influence in our children's spiritual lives I couldn't say," says Sally Heath. "In their earliest years, taking them to church regularly was more out of habit than it was out of deep faith."

Sally explains:

That was the case until one Saturday in January of 1972, while attending a women's seminar in a church in Anchorage (thanks to my friend Mary Ellan Moe).

There must have been an invitation to find a new life in Christ and I responded to that invitation. It was instantaneous—the cleansing, forgiveness, and renewal I experienced. Even after years of required Saturday confessions and penances, there was nothing equal to confessing directly to God and the feeling that I was beginning a brand-new life. I had known nothing about the Bible, never even read it, but from that day on I longed to read and understand everything in it. It's as real to me today as it was then.

When I returned home to Wasilla I joyfully called a priest to describe the experience and was told, "Be careful. It sounds like the strange phenomenon happening around the country." I didn't know what he was talking about.

I went back to work the next evening. At that time, I was the secretary for a Presbyterian minister. I couldn't wait to tell him about what had happened, and he, too, was quite unimpressed.

Eventually, I called Paul and Helen Riley, ministers of the Assembly of God Church, and they immediately came over and understood completely what I was talking about. The kids and I began attending there and were baptized by Pastor Riley in 1975. Sarah and her brother and sisters had been baptized as infants but once they realized what it was all about, they asked for baptism "like the Bible says."

We attended there for many years and then, as they were all out on their own, we all began attending other equally fine churches.

Only Sarah can speak of her own faith, but I can say, assuredly, that her faith is deep and profound, and her love of God, family, and country is real.

Mary Ellan Moe tells this story about Sally Heath and her family:

When I met Sally, she was such a wonderful person, it was hard to tell she wasn't a Christian. Some people are like that—they seem to have more innate goodness than many of us who are believers.

Sally had been reading a copy of *Good News for Modern Man* at a campfire while we were on an outing, so it was apparent that she was searching. My husband suggested I invite Sally to the upcoming women's seminar at our Anchorage church. I thought that was a great idea, and I did just that.

That day came, and we spent it together. I remember that Sally experienced a lot of joy and tears during the retreat, and it was wonderful to share in that experience with her.

We have been friends for about 37 years now, and our families have shared many great times together, from home Bible studies to skiing and hunting, to hiking the Chilkoot Trail; to dinners and birthdays and holidays.

In those early years, friends were like family in Alaska because most of us didn't have family living nearby. We enjoyed her children immensely, following their basketball games, and are still close to her girls.

Sarah Heath made a personal commitment to Christ at age 12. Her faith has remained a steady and meaningful part of her life ever since that time.

While she was in high school, she led a group of the Fellowship of Christian Athletes. With her strong faith influences and friends of like mind, Sarah grew stronger. She sought out believers in her college years as well.

Today, Sarah Palin often identifies herself simply as "Christian." She believes in the integrity of the Scripture, lives her life by it, and prays for guidance and God's wisdom in her life. Sarah does not put name tags on what she believes. She simply practices Christian morals and integrity.

As Alaska governor, she signed a proclamation honoring Christian Heritage Week and said creationism should also be taught in the schools alongside evolution and science.

Today, social and Christian conservatives form a large part of her support base. Faith and values are the large part of discussions about Sarah. Her Barracuda tenacity keeps a strong faith and commitment to integrity in all she does.

In 2002, Sarah joined the Wasilla Bible Church, a nondenominational evangelical church that, according to its statement of faith: *believes in the Bible as the inspired inerrant Word of God authoritative for faith and practice.* When she's in the state capital, Sarah attends the Juneau Christian Center.

Lieutenant Governor Sean Parnell, Governor Sarah Palin, and U.S. Senator Lisa Murkowski receive a blessing from Pastor Ed Kalnins at One Lord Sunday in the Mat-Su Valley.

CHAPTER 4

"Toddy for the Body"

Todd was born to Jim Palin and Blanche Kalstrom (Jim's first wife) on September 6, 1964, in Dillingham, Alaska. Todd Mitchell Palin entered a world he was destined to help change.

Todd was raised in Alaska's rural terrain. This inspired in him a love for the outdoors. His grandparents, Alfred and Helena Andree, had a great impact on him. This influence was far-reaching, shaping the man he would become. Todd is a true Alaskan, and has always made his home there. He is part Yup'ik Eskimo.

Sarah Heath and Todd Palin a few months before their August 1988 marriage.

Sarah married Todd, her high school sweetheart, on

Sarah and Todd's then-new car.

Sarah and Todd at their 1982 prom.

August 29, 1988. They eloped shortly after Todd graduated from college, and when they learned they needed witnesses for the civil ceremony, they went down the street to the retirement home to find two willing participants.

Although Governor Sarah Palin refers to Todd as the "First Dude," he likes people to call him "Todd," but doesn't mind the nickname.

Todd is a pilot (he owns a Piper PA-18 Super Cub), moose-hunter, salmon fisherman (he owns a commercial fishing business), and four-time champion of the Torso Iron Dog—the world's longest snow machine race.

In September of 2008, Todd was asked about difficulties with extreme temperatures. He said sometimes he's had to deal with temperatures that are "minus 80 below, with some wind chill factor on top. You just prepare for it, you know." He explained. "If it's raining outside, you put rain gear on. If you're on the slope working and it's 40 below, you bundle up and you make sure that, you know, you're going to be safe ... They've got some great technology out there as far as clothing and protection."

Todd Palin is in the limelight, yet he makes you feel like you could walk right up to him, shake his hand, and instantly have the rapport you have with a childhood buddy. From all appearances, he handles himself with poise and is hard-working, loyal, and personable.

Todd's Grandma Andree—dressed in a kuspuk—*is Yup'ik Eskimo.*

TODDY FOR THE BODY

Todd's cousin, Deanna, a student at New Mexico State University, shared this story:

This is my third year at NMSU, and I'm real proud to be related to Sarah Palin. Todd Palin is my cousin. My immediate family all live in Homer and the Iliamna area. My Grandma Andree is also Todd's Grandma. After Sarah suddenly was thrust into the limelight we (started calling) Grandma Andree, "The First Grandma."

There isn't another soul more proud of Sarah then our Grandma, and she makes sure she watches everything that is on TV (and the reruns) with Sarah in it. Grandma Andree keeps up on all the politicians and past presidents. She loves it all. Gram even prays for the president and our country everyday.

Our family has always kept in contact with everyone—Todd's family, JD's, and Kristi's—through Grandma. After the GOP convention speech from Sarah, we got a phone call from Todd. He was so excited; you could just hear it in his voice when he called. We were all still talking about how wonderful Sarah was when the phone rang and it was Todd asking us what we thought. Of course we told Todd that Piper

Left to right: *Track, Grandma Andree, Bristol, Todd and Willow*

stole the show with the sweetest lick, and he really laughed about that. Gram was the one he wanted to speak to and, of course, that truly made her day.

Grandma is Yup'ik Eskimo and is from the Dillingham area, so she took care of the kids when they were young. Auntie Blanche (Todd's Mom) worked for AFN (Alaska Federation of Natives) and traveled a lot, so Grandma came in handy as a babysitter. Grandpa Andree also babysat and cared for the kids. That's when he gave Todd a nickname, "Toddy for the Body." Now, whenever we see Todd on TV we say, there's our Toddy for the Body.

A year ago Grandma made a decision to move in with us and we are happy to have our "First Grandma" so close by.

Raising a Family

The newly wedded Todd and Sarah Palin started their family right away.

Track C.J. Palin was born just a year after Todd and Sarah married. Track is in the National Guard and at the time of this writing is soon to be deployed to Iraq. Daughters Bristol—named after Todd and Sarah's favorite fishing bay—and Willow—named for the Alaskan state bird, the Willow Ptarmigan—were born in 1990 and 1994, respectively.

In 2001, Piper Indy, another baby girl was born. Piper was named after Todd's beloved Piper PA-18 plane and his snowmobile, a Polaris Indy.

In 2008, Trig Paxson Van was born. Trig was born with Down-Syndrome. According to AlbertMohler.com, "As soon as Todd was told about it, he quickly said, 'We shouldn't be asking, "Why us?" We should be saying, "Well, why not us?"'"

In the political forefront, Sarah and her family are under constant scrutiny. They have proved who they are in character. This family is dedicated, tough, and loyal. Through tough times and good times, they have loved and supported one another, while managing to stay grounded.

Chapter 5

An Effective Leader

Sarah Palin's accomplishments don't begin with being voted into public office. They began when she was a child and became more visible during her high school athletic days. Here are some of those accomplishments:

• Fellowship of Christian Athletes: A member in high school.

• Miss Alaska: Runner up. Knowing she might win a scholarship if she could win in the Miss Alaska Pageant, Sarah gave it a try. Her hope turned into reality; she won a college scholarship and the "Miss Congeniality" award.

- City Council: 1992-1996 (served two terms)

This time in local office served to stir in Sarah a dissatisfaction with current politics and governing tactics. She could have been swayed, but instead of letting go and joining the status quo, she proceeded to pursue places where she could have greater influence and help the people more.

- Mayor of Wasilla: 1996-2002 (served two terms)

In October 1996, Palin became mayor and was responsible for a $6 million budget with 53 employees. She began to make staffing changes. She eliminated the position of museum director and asked for updated resumes and resignation letters from Wasilla police chief, Irl Stambaugh; public works director, Jack Felton; finance director, Duane Dvorak; and librarian, Mary Ellen Emmons.

She temporarily required department heads to get her approval before talking to reporters, stating they first needed to become better acquainted with her policies. As promised during her campaign, she reduced her own salary from $68,000 to $64,000; she also reduced her workload by hiring a new city administrator, resulting in an overall increase in the budget. State Republican Party leaders began grooming her for higher office, and despite a rocky start, Sarah gained popularity with Wasilla voters. She kept a jar full of names of Wasilla residents on her desk, and once a week she would pull out a name and call them, asking them how they thought the city was doing.

- President of Alaska Conference of Mayors: 1999

Palin was elected by her peers to serve as president of the Alaska Conference of Mayors. In this role, she worked with local, state, and federal officials to promote solutions to the needs of Alaska's communities.

- Chair of the Alaska Oil and Gas Conservation Commission: 2003-2004

- Governor of Alaska: Inaugurated on December 4, 2006

History was made on December 4, 2006. Sarah Palin became the 11th governor of Alaska, and the first woman to hold the office. At age 42, she was also the youngest governor in Alaskan history. She is the first governor to have been born after Alaska achieved U.S. statehood, and the first not to be inaugurated in Juneau; she chose to have the ceremony held in Fairbanks instead. She took office on December 4, 2006, and has maintained a high approval rating throughout her term. Palin declared that top priorities of her administration would be resource development, education, and work-force development, public health and safety, and transportation and infrastructure development.

One of the remarkable facts surrounding the accomplishment of being elected to Governor of Alaska is in her grassroots campaign. It was comprised of dedicated, hard-working people. These people, though ordinary, were extraordinary—and they were people who simply wanted change. She lacked the money, but not the manpower, to spread her name. And her victory was not hers alone, but it was also a victory for the common people.

• Chair of the Interstate Oil and Gas Compact Commission

A multi-state government agency that promotes the conservation and efficient recovery of domestic oil and natural gas resources while protecting health, safety, and the environment.

• Chair of the National Governors Association (NGA) Natural Resources Committee

Charged with pursuing legislation to ensure state needs are considered as federal policy is formulated in the areas of agriculture, energy, environmental protection, and natural-resource management. Prior to being named to this position, she served as co-chair of this committee.

• Republican Nominee for Vice-President of the United States: 2008

In August of 2008, Sarah Palin became the first female Republican nominee for Vice-president of the United States. She was selected by John McCain, the Republican candidate for President of the United States.

CHAPTER 6

Dodge the Issues? No Way!

This chapter contains quotes, proclamations, interviews, and news articles that help reveal where Sarah Palin stands on the issues that concern all Americans. All excerpts are used by permission of the various agencies and publications.

ABORTION, ADOPTION, AND BIRTH CONTROL

"I'm pro-life. I'll do all I can to see every baby is created with a future and potential. The legislature should do all it can to protect human life."

Source: Q and A with Newsmax.com's Mike Coppock, August 29, 2008.

According to an October 2006 profile in the *Anchorage Daily News*, Palin opposes stem-cell research, physician-assisted suicide, and state health benefits for same-sex partners.

Source: *Anchorage Daily News*, October, 2007.

Safe Haven.

Governor Palin Signs "Safe Haven" Bill Into Law: Bill allows parents to surrender newborns without prosecution.

Palin signed House Bill 29 into law today. The "Safe Haven for Infants Act" passed the State House in May and passed the Senate on Jan. 19. The bill allows a parent to safely surrender a newborn child without the threat of prosecution, as long as there is no evidence the infant has been physically injured.

Without penalty, a parent may leave the infant in the physical custody of a peace officer, physician or hospital employee, or a volunteer or employee of a fire station or emergency medical service. "All children deserve to begin their lives in a loving, protective family," Governor Palin said. "When that fails, it is our job as a state to make sure that children are protected."

The Commissioner of Health and Social Services said, "Unfortunately, abandonment of infants has occurred in Alaska. It is our hope that the passage of the 'Safe Haven' act has ended that forever."

Source: Alaska Governor's Office: Press release 08-020, "Safe Haven," February 11, 2008.

Adoption.

• WHEREAS, there is nothing more important to Alaska than the safe growth, development, and nurturance of Alaska's children. It is our children who will determine the direction of Alaska in future years.

- WHEREAS, Alaska has 847 children living in out-of-home care who cannot return to their birth parents and need the security, encouragement, safety, and cultural continuity that a permanent family can provide.

- WHEREAS, adoption is the plan for permanency for these children. In 2006, 226 children from foster care achieved finalized adoption with families in Alaska.

- WHEREAS, children waiting for adoptive parents and adoptive families require and deserve community and agency support.

- NOW, THEREFORE, I, Sarah Palin, Governor of the State of Alaska, do hereby proclaim November 2007 as Adoption Awareness Month in Alaska, and encourage all Alaskans to become involved in community and state efforts to provide all our children with secure, nurturing, permanent families.

Source: Alaska Governor's Office: Proclamation, "Adoption," October 22, 2007.

If Roe v. Wade got overturned …

Q: If Roe v. Wade were overturned and states could once again prohibit abortion, in your view, to what extent should abortion be prohibited in Alaska?

A: Under this hypothetical scenario, it would not be up to the governor to unilaterally ban anything. It would be up to the people of Alaska to discuss and decide how we would like our society to reflect our values.

Source: *Anchorage Daily News*: 2006 gubernatorial candidate profile, October 22, 2006.

Publicly funded abortions.

A: I oppose the use of public funds for elective abortions.

Source: *Anchorage Daily News*: 2006 gubernatorial candidate profile, October 22, 2006.

Pro-contraception, pro-woman, pro-life.

What about the social issues that Alaskans, especially the party faithful who often decide primary elections, may find important? Here's what Sarah Palin has to say about abortion.

Palin said last month that no woman should have to choose between her career, education and her child. She is pro-contraception and said she's a member of a pro-woman but anti-abortion group called Feminists for Life. "I believe in the strength and the power of women, and the potential of every human life," she said.

Source: *Anchorage Daily News*, "Little Play," by K. Hopkins, August 6, 2006.

BUDGET AND THE ECONOMY

Control spending.

"I got rid of a few things in the governor's office that I didn't believe our citizens should have to pay for. That luxury jet [for personal use by the governor] was over the top. I put it on eBay. I also drive myself to work.

"And I thought we could muddle through without the governor's personal chef—although I've got to admit that sometimes my kids sure miss her. I came to office promising to control spending—by request if possible and by veto if necessary."

Source: Speech at 2008 Republican National Convention, September 3, 2008.

Funding education and transportation.

Keeping her commitment to save for the future, Governor Sarah Palin today announced details of a two-year $7.1 billion savings plan. "We are celebrating a milestone in Alaska's history—an opportunity to save for the future and work toward a more predictable budget," said Governor Palin. The two-year savings plan calls for:

• Investing $2.6 billion in the Education Fund to help fund public education in the future.

• Creating a $1 billion fund whose earnings would be used for future transportation infrastructure.

• Replenishing the Constitutional Budget Reserve with $379 million.

• Investing $250 million in an alternative energy fund. This fund would be used for energy projects recommended by a strategic energy plan, which could include hydroelectric, wind, geothermal, biomass and tidal power.

• Governor Palin also proposes to deposit $2.4 billion from the Permanent Fund earnings reserve to the Permanent Fund principal.

Source: Alaska Governor's Office: Press release 07-233, "Savings," December 5, 2007.

Reduce general fund spending.

Governor Palin is committed to a budget that controls the growth of government, forces the state to live within its means, and encourages healthy savings for the state's future. The governor's budget includes funding to restore the longevity bonus program, a community revenue sharing program and fully funds the education foundation formula. From the moment Governor Palin took office, she directed all state agencies to look for efficiencies and savings. Through a collective effort, the governor was able to reduce general fund spending in the operating budget alone by over $124 million. The capital budget maximizes federal funding and focuses on the administration's priorities. The governor will continue to work with the legislature to craft a final budget that meets the needs of Alaskans.

Source: Alaska Governor's Office: press release, "100th Day," March 13, 2007.

Aim to reduce general fund spending by $150 million.

"I have established an aggressive goal of reducing general fund spending by $150 million dollars. This takes tremendous effort by staff as well as the cooperation of the Legislature. On the savings side, by depositing our one-time surplus of $1.8 billion dollars, we'll build our savings account to nearly $4.3 billion dollars. It's a necessary step to ensure that we can fund essential services tomorrow; and avoid massive 'single year' cuts down the road, if and when, faced with tougher times."

Source: State of the State Address, January 17, 2007.

Firm believer in free-market capitalism.

"I am a conservative Republican, a firm believer in free market capitalism. A free-market system allows all parties to compete, which ensures the best and most competitive project emerges, and ensures a fair, democratic process.

"I will communicate progress on gas line negotiations to the public. My administration will pursue the plan that is best for ALL Alaskans. All qualified and viable proposals and applicants will be considered."

Source: Palin-Parnell campaign booklet: *New Energy for Alaska,* November 3, 2006.

Coordinate state tourism marketing without additional funding.

The next governor also will help shape how the legislature will spend the anticipated tens of millions in new cruise-tax revenue.

Knowles said he would work with the legislature to use a portion of the new cruise tax revenue to market Alaskan tourism. The candidate complains that the state's funding for tourism marketing has plunged in the last decade. "When you compare that to other states, like Connecticut, Indiana or Tennessee, we're out-marketed across the board," Knowles said in a recent interview. Knowles said he supports doubling state funding for tourism marketing to $10 million.

Palin said the state should continue to match industry's marketing funds, but a "huge overblown budget" isn't necessary to entice more travelers to

Alaska. "It doesn't necessarily cost more money to market," Palin said at the recent Wasilla gubernatorial debate. She advocated for "better coordination" and "better ideas" as the way to improve tourism marketing.

Source: *Anchorage Daily News*: 2006 gubernatorial candidate profile, October 30, 2006.

CIVIL RIGHTS

Recognized Juneteenth to celebrate the end of slavery.

• WHEREAS, Juneteenth is an annual holiday commemorating the ending of slavery—the oldest celebration of its kind. Its roots go back to June 19, 1865, when Union soldiers arrived in Galveston, Texas to announce the war's end and that all slaves were now free. That news took two and a half years after President Lincoln's Emancipation Proclamation, which had become official January 1, 1863.

• WHEREAS, today, Juneteenth is a day, a week, and in some areas, a month that is set aside to celebrate African American freedom.

• WHEREAS, in cities across the country, people of all races, nationalities, and religions are joining together to celebrate this extremely important historical event.

• NOW, THEREFORE, I, Sarah Palin, Governor of the State of Alaska, do hereby proclaim June 21, 2008, as Juneteenth Day in Alaska, and encourage all Alaskans to reflect on the importance of this celebration, and encourage citizens to take part in the events taking place in your communities.

Source: Alaska Governor's Office: Proclamation, "Juneteenth," June 17, 2008.

HIV/AIDS among Alaska Natives is public health crisis.

- WHEREAS, American Indians and Alaska Natives have experienced a long history of a lower health status, which includes a lower life expectancy and higher disease occurrence than other racial/ethnic groups due to inadequate health education, disproportionate poverty, discrimination in the delivery of health care services, and access to quality health care.

- WHEREAS, the spread of HIV/AIDS virus among American Indians and Alaska Natives poses a significant risk to the public health and well-being of these communities.

- WHEREAS, the status of HIV/AIDS epidemic among American Indians and Alaska Natives is a public health crisis that requires a focused national effort as well as tribal effort to bring attention to the prevention needs of Indigenous people.

- NOW THEREFORE, I, Governor Sarah Palin, do hereby proclaim March 20, 2008, as: Native HIV/ AIDS Awareness Day in Alaska, and ask the residents of Alaska to observe this day with appropriate programs and activities.

Source: Alaska Governor's Office: Proclamation, "Native HIV," March 4, 2008.

Recognizes Martin Luther King holiday.

• WHEREAS, as we observe the birthday of Dr. Martin Luther King, Jr., we remember the dream of a great man—an American hero—and his message of social change through nonviolence.

• WHEREAS, Dr. King dedicated his life to empowering people, no matter their circumstances, and challenged them to lift up their neighbors and communities. He broke down barriers within our society by encouraging Americans to look past their differences and refused to rest until our Nation fulfilled its pledge of liberty and justice for all.

• WHEREAS, Alaskans will join volunteers across the nation who will celebrate Dr. King's life and teachings by converting the holiday into a day of service, dedicated to meeting community needs.

• WHEREAS, yet more work remains. In the words of Dr. King, "We will not be satisfied until 'justice rolls down like waters and righteousness like a mighty stream.'"

• NOW, THEREFORE, I, Governor Sarah Palin, do hereby proclaim January 21, 2008, as Dr. Martin Luther King, Jr. Day in Alaska.

Source: Alaska Governor's Office: Proclamation, "MLK Day," January 14, 2008.

Comply with same-sex partner benefits despite disagreement.

Governor Sarah Palin today announced that, per the recent ruling of the Supreme Court of Alaska, the State of Alaska's regulations are in effect to begin providing state benefits to same-sex partners beginning January 1, 2007. "The Supreme Court has ordered adoption of the regulations by the State of Alaska to begin providing benefits January 1," said Governor Palin. "We have no more judicial options. We may disagree with the rationale behind the ruling, but our responsibility is to proceed forward with the law and follow the Constitution."

In addition to adoption of the regulations, Governor Palin signed HB4002 today, which calls for a statewide advisory vote, proposed by the legislature during its November special session. "I disagree with the recent court decision because I feel as though Alaskans spoke on this issue with its overwhelming support for a Constitutional Amendment in 1998 which defined marriage as between a man and woman. But the Supreme Court has spoken and the state will abide.

Source: Alaska Governor's Office: Press release 06-012, "Same-Sex," December 20, 2006.

Marriage is only be only between and man and a woman.

I am pro-life, and I believe that marriage should only be between and man and a woman.

Source: Campaign website, www.palinforgovernor.com, "Issues," November 7, 2006.

Value our cultural diversity.

Sarah Palin and Sean Parnell are a New Team with New Energy for Alaska who value our cultural diversity and will provide opportunities for all Alaskans.

Source: Palin-Parnell campaign booklet: *New Energy for Alaska.* November 3, 2006.

Deny benefits to homosexual couples.

Here's what Sarah Palin has to say about same-sex marriage. Palin said she's not out to judge anyone and has good friends who are gay, but that she supported the 1998 constitutional amendment.

Elected officials can't defy the court when it comes to how rights are applied, she said, but she would support a ballot question that would deny benefits to homosexual couples. "I believe that honoring the family structure is that important," Palin said. She said she doesn't know if people choose to be gay.

Source: *Anchorage Daily News*, "Little Play," by K. Hopkins, August 6, 2006.

Q: Do you support the Alaska Supreme Court's ruling that spousal benefits for state employees should be given to same-sex couples?

A: No, I believe spousal benefits are reserved for married citizens, as defined in our constitution.

Source: Eagle Forum 2006 Gubernatorial Candidate Questionnaire, July 31, 2006.

Top priorities include preserving definition of "marriage."

Q: In relationship to families, what are your top three priorities if elected governor?

A: 1. Creating an atmosphere where parents feel welcome to choose the venues of education for their children.

2. Preserving the definition of "marriage," as it is defined in our constitution.

3. Cracking down on the things that harm family life: gangs, drug use, and infringement of our liberties including attacks on our 2nd Amendment rights.

Source: Eagle Forum 2006 Gubernatorial Candidate Questionnaire, July 31, 2006.

CORPORATIONS

Encourage small-business growth by reducing business taxes.

"Alaska's small-business owners are the backbone of our regional economies. Small Alaskan-owned businesses should have just as much say in state policy as the big companies do. Our precious businesses are major employers of Alaskans and keep Alaska's money circulating through our economy. As Mayor and CEO of the booming city of Wasilla, my team invited investment and encouraged business growth by eliminating small business inventory taxes, eliminated personal property taxes, reduced real property tax mill levies every year I was in office, reduced fees, and built the infrastructure our businesses needed to grow and prosper."

Source: Palin-Parnell campaign booklet: *New Energy for Alaska.* November 3, 2006.

CRIME

Establish "FBI Day" to support the fight against global crime.

- WHEREAS, the FBI commemorates its 100th anniversary this month;
- WHEREAS, the FBI's mission is to defend America from global terrorism and global crime, while at all times upholding our civil liberties;
- WHEREAS, thanks to the rise of globalization, crime and terrorism can cross international boundaries with a single keystroke;
- WHEREAS, the FBI is not just facing kidnapers, gangsters, and thieves—it is facing terrorists, spies, hackers, violent gangs, international organized crime syndicates, corrupt corporations and public officials, and those who traffic in weapons, narcotics, and even human beings;
- WHEREAS, the FBI has more than 90 dedicated FBI agents and professional support employees who serve in Alaska.
- NOW, THEREFORE, I, Sarah Palin, Governor of the State of Alaska, do hereby proclaim July 26, 2008, as FBI Day in Alaska, and encourage Alaskans to wish the FBI a happy 100-year anniversary.

Source: Alaska Governor's Office: Proclamation, "FBI Day," June 12, 2008.

Register sex offenders and investigate internet sex crimes.

Governor Palin today signed Senate Bill 265 into law. During the legislative session, several crime bills, including the governor's crime bill, were rolled into SB 265. SB 265 bars convicted sex offenders from receiving a permanent fund dividend [Alaska state tax rebate] if they fail to keep their information current on the state Sex Offender Registry, [among other changes] to the criminal codes.

"I thank legislators who helped craft this comprehensive approach to strengthening public safety," Governor Palin said. "These are good steps toward sound public safety policy. We must continue to meet the needs of law enforcement and the judicial system to keep our citizens safe." Senate Bill 265 also:

• Makes a third offense for bootlegging within 15 years a class C felony.

• Allows the state to pursue court-ordered restitution from anyone convicted of unlawfully taking game.

• Funds a special investigator, prosecutor, and computer technician to detect and prosecute internet sex crimes.

Source: Alaska Governor's Office: Press release, "Crime Bill," June 5, 2008.

Victims' rights are critical to "justice for all."

• WHEREAS, Alaska has made great strides in ensuring crime victims are treated with dignity and respect. Victims' rights are a critical component of the promise of "justice for all," the foundation for America's justice system.

• WHEREAS, crime victims in Alaska have protections and guaranties under the Alaska State Constitution, but we must do better to strive to protect, expand, and observe crime victims' rights so that there truly is justice for victims and justice for all.

• NOW, THEREFORE, I, Sarah Palin, Governor of the State of Alaska, do hereby proclaim April 13-19, 2008, as Crime Victims' Rights Week in Alaska, and reaffirm this state's commitment to strive to reach the goal of justice for all by ensuring that all victims are afforded their legal rights and provided with assistance as they face the financial, physical, and psychological impact of crime.

Source: Alaska Governor's Office: Proclamation, "Crime Victims," March 18, 2008.

Get tough on crime and beef up law enforcement.

"In Public Safety and Corrections, after years of positions left vacant, we've doubled academy recruits. We're building public trust by demanding the highest standards of those in public safety. We're implementing realistic plans to deal with overcrowded prisons, including rehabilitation and work requirements for the 95 percent of inmates who will re-enter society instead of just 'warehousing' them. In Law, we are getting tough on criminals with tougher, defensible sentences. It was a clean sweep for convictions in the Cold Case Unit. Our Civil Division is managing hundreds of legal battles to protect Alaskans' interests. I commend Law for last year's needed, comprehensive ethics bill. In Military and Veterans Affairs, we certified hundreds of territorial guardsmen, so those who served finally receive their benefits. We are proudly supporting our brave Alaska Guard as they provide daily search and rescue in our State, and support the War on Terror."

Source: State of the State Address to the 25th Alaska Legislature, January 15, 2008.

Collect DNA samples from felons.

The governor today signed House Bill 90, the Omnibus Crime Bill, which strengthens laws dealing with violent offenders, sexual predators, prostitution, people who witness a violent crime and fail to report it, and people who have been ordered not to consume alcohol. The bill also allows police in Alaska to collect a DNA sample from adults arrested for a felony or a crime against another person.

Source: Alaska Governor's Office: Press release 07-156, "Signing," June 25, 2007.

Gang members on probation must wear electronic monitors.

The governor today signed House Bill 133, which requires people who are convicted of violent, gang-related crimes to wear electronic monitoring devices as a condition of their probation. This will allow law enforcement officials to monitor the movement of violent offenders and supervise their activity.

Source: Alaska Governor's Office: Press release 07-156, "Signing," June 25, 2007.

Maximum sentence for first-degree murder by police.

Governor Sarah Palin today signed Senate Bill 45, the Sonya Ivanoff Act. SB 45 mandates the maximum sentence for first-degree murder when committed by an on-duty peace officer.

Sonya Ivanoff, 19, was murdered in 2003, by a Nome police officer. Matthew Owens was convicted of first-degree murder and sentenced to 99 years in prison. His case is currently on appeal.

Governor Palin was joined at the bill signing ceremony by Sonya's parents and siblings. "The inappropriate actions of Matthew Owens cloud the focus and the image of our brave men and women who have all sworn to protect and serve," said Governor Palin. "We must work with all our communities in a trusting partnership to ensure that every citizen feels safe, and is treated fairly and with respect."

Source: Alaska Governor's Office: Press release, "SB45, Sonya," April 27, 2007.

Supports the death penalty and public safety presence, via police, courts, and prisons.

I support adequate funding for a strong public safety presence in Alaska. Feeling safe in our communities is something we cannot accept any compromise on. This includes policing in all its forms, the court system, prosecutors and corrections. If the legislature passed a death-penalty law, I would sign it. We have a right to know that someone who rapes and murders a child or kills an innocent person in a drive-by shooting will never be able to do that again.

Source: Campaign website, www.palinforgovernor.com, "Issues," November 7, 2006.

Death penalty for adults who murder children.

Q: Would you introduce—or, if introduced by a legislator, would you support—a bill to adopt the death penalty in Alaska? If yes, which crimes should it apply to?

A: If the Legislature were to pass a bill that established a death penalty on adults who murder children, I would sign it.

Source: *Anchorage Daily News*: 2006 gubernatorial candidate profile, October 22, 2006.

No hate-crime legislation.

Q: Will you support an effort to expand hate-crime laws?

A: No, as I believe all heinous crime is based on hate.

Source: Eagle Forum 2006 Gubernatorial Candidate
Questionnaire, July 31, 2006.

No expansion of gambling in Alaska.

Q: Do you support the expansion of gambling in
Alaska?

A: No, in so many cases, gambling has shown ill
effects on families and as governor I would not propose
expansion legislation.

Q: Would you sign any bills that expand gaming in
our state?

A: No.

Source: Eagle Forum 2006 Gubernatorial Candidate
Questionnaire, July 31, 2006.

Drugs and Alcohol

Supports strict drunk-driving laws.

Keeping Alaskans safe on our highways is a top
priority of my administration. I'm pleased to report
highway fatalities in Alaska are down this year. Since
July 28, Alaska has recorded 34 fatalities for the entire
year of 2008, and that number is below the decade-
average of 46 at this point in the calendar year. Strict
enforcement of laws regulating drunk driving, reckless
driving and seatbelt use have contributed to this positive
news.

Source: Alaska Governor's Office: August 2008 Newsletter,
August 20, 2008.

Maintain alcohol sale database.

The governor today signed two alcohol-related bills. Senate Bill 128 is aimed at preventing bootleggers from ordering alcohol from numerous package stores in violation of local option. SB 128 requires the ABC Board, in conjunction with package store licensees, to maintain a database documenting the sale, distribution, and purchase of alcoholic beverages, ordered in writing, from people living in damp local-option communities.

The governor also signed House Bill 118, sponsored by Representative Kevin Meyer. The bill closes a gap in statute by making it a non-criminal violation to permit underage people to possess alcohol in your home. Under current law (AS 04.16.050), a parent who allows their own child to possess alcohol is not subject to the violation because they are allowed to provide alcohol to their children. Under HB 118, however, a person throwing a party where an underage person possesses alcohol, even if they were not responsible for providing the alcohol, would face a $500 fine.

Source: Alaska Governor's Office: Press release 07-156, "Signing," June 25, 2007.

Questions cruise-ship gambling under casino gambling ban.

Palin questioned business aspects of the new cruise-ship law in an October 17 letter to the Alaska Travel Industry Association, the state's major tourism group: "We all have to recognize that voters passed the measure—it is water under the bridge—but now we have to work together to make sure that it doesn't have a negative impact on you—as small business owners," Palin wrote.

Palin worried about the law's new tax on gambling while ships are in state waters. "Currently casino gambling is prohibited in Alaska. So what are we getting ourselves into?" Palin also asked.

Though she didn't say how she would do it, Palin told the ATIA she would work with the tourism industry to "mitigate some of the impacts" from the new law. Knowles spokeswoman Patty Ginsburg said Friday that her boss supported taxing the cruise industry but he was unhappy with the law's other provisions.

Source: *Anchorage Daily News*: 2006 gubernatorial candidate profile, October 30, 2006.

Crack down on gang activity.

Q: In relationship to families, what are your top three priorities if elected governor?

A: 1. Creating an atmosphere where parents feel welcome to choose the venues of education for their children.

2. Preserving the definition of "marriage," as defined in our constitution.

3. Cracking down on the things that harm family life: gangs, drug use, and infringement of our liberties, including attacks on our 2nd Amendment rights.

Source: Eagle Forum 2006 Gubernatorial Candidate Questionnaire, July 31, 2006.

EDUCATION

Supports teaching intelligent design in public schools.

Palin is a conservative Protestant and has also been a member since 2006 of Feminists for Life, an anti-abortion group. She has supported the teaching of intelligent design in public schools, alongside evolution. She is a member of the National Rifle Association, and has said Alaska's economic future depends on aggressively extracting its vast natural resources, from oil to natural gas and minerals.

Source: *New York Times*, pp. A1 and A10, "An Outsider Who Charms," August 29, 2008.

Supports No Child Left Behind.

Congratulations to the staff at the 294 Alaska public schools that made adequate yearly progress under the federal No Child Left Behind (NCLB) standards for the 2007-2008 school year. Our schools faced a higher bar in 2007-2008 for the percentages of students who score proficient in language arts and math assessments. Congratulations to the many schools that continue to improve in student achievement but may have fallen short in 1 or 2 of the 31 categories schools are held accountable for in NCLB.

Source: Alaska Governor's Office: August 2008 Newsletter, August 20, 2008.

School debate should focus on accountability.

In education, we are shaping a three-year funding plan to finally shift the school debate from perpetual "money talk" to accountability and achievement! We are focusing on foundational skills needed in the "real-world" workplace and in college.

Source: State of the State Address to the 25th Alaska Legislature, January 15, 2008.

Committed to providing strong education, including morals education.

It is our energy development that pays for essential services, like education. Victor Hugo said, "He who opens a school door, closes a prison." It's a privileged obligation we have to "open education doors." Every child, of every ability, is to be cherished and loved and taught. Every child provides this world hope. They are the most beautiful ingredient in our sometimes muddied-up world. I am committed to our children and their education. Stepping through "the door" is about more than passing a standardized test. We need kids prepared to pass life's tests—like getting a job and valuing a strong work ethic. Our Three-year Education Plan invests more than a billion dollars each year. We must forward-fund education, letting schools plan ahead. We must stop pink-slipping teachers, and then struggle to recruit and retain them the next year.

Source: State of the State Address to the 25th Alaska Legislature, January 15, 2008.

Budget funds for education and job training.

"We're asking lawmakers to pass a new K-12 funding plan this year. This is an investment that is needed to increase the base student allocation, district cost factors, and intensive needs students. It includes $100 million in school construction and deferred maintenance. There is awesome potential to improve education and embrace choice for parents. This potential will prime Alaska to compete in a global economy. Beyond high school, we will boost job training and university options. We are proposing more than $10 million in new funding for apprenticeship programs, expansion of construction, engineering and health care degrees. But it must be about more than funds, it must be a change in philosophy. It is time to shift focus, from just dollars to 'caliyulriit,' which is Yupik for 'people who want to work.' Work for pride in supporting our families. It's about results and getting kids excited about their future—whether it is college, trade school or ..."

Source: State of the State Address to the 25th Alaska Legislature, January 15, 2008.

Court ruling against NEA: state adequately funds education.

Alaska has "fully met its constitutional obligation to adequately fund education," an Anchorage Superior Court ruled today in the case of Moore vs. Alaska. The plaintiffs—which included NEA-Alaska and several school districts—sued the state, asking the court to order significantly more state funding for Alaska schools—seeking to double Alaska's education budget.

Instead, the judge left decisions about the state's education-funding formula to the legislature, and said the court would not determine educational programs. The judge's ruling said the evidence shows that Alaska has "thorough and appropriate" educational standards and a "finely tuned" method of testing children.

But the state must be more aggressive in overseeing troubled school districts, the judge ruled, citing the Yupiit School District, one of the plaintiffs, in particular. In those schools, the court also found that students haven't had sufficient opportunity to prepare for the high school exit exam.

Source: Alaska Governor's Office: Press release 07-154 "Court Rules," June 21, 2007.

Fully fund K-12 and support early funding of education.

"My budget includes fully funding the 'K through 12' foundation formula. In addition, I've included more than $200 million in new dollars to cover the increased retirement costs for local school districts, so that more local school district dollars get into the classroom, where the money belongs. We're facing a potential $10 billion PERS/TRS retirement plan shortfall that affects local schools. Our $200-million-dollar line item for school districts is part of the half BILLION dollar proposal to help the districts, local governments, and the state alleviate the pension-plan burden while we work with the legislature on a long-term solution. I've also committed to help provide local school districts with more predictability, for better planning by supporting 'early funding of education.' I'll introduce a separate education appropriation bill and ask that it's passed. Our local school districts deserve to know what they have to work with early enough for them to create efficiencies through planning.

Source: State of the State Address to the 24th Alaska Legislature, January 17, 2007.

Supports $20 million needs-based aid for University of Alaska.

We have no needs-based aid for Alaska students. Governor Murkowski tried to put $20 million in the budget for aid, but the legislature rejected it. Let's make our own university available to students who might otherwise go without higher education.

Source: Palin-Parnell campaign booklet: *New Energy for Alaska*. November 3, 2006.

Forward-fund K-12 schools to allow better planning.

"I support adequate and full funding for education, as well as for pupil transportation and municipal school-debt reimbursements. There must be recognition for increases in costs for energy, utilities, insurance, and salaries. We cannot go back to the day of simply ignoring inflation. A centerpiece of my fiscal plan is to forward fund K-12. School districts will be able to do a better job of planning their budgets for upcoming years if they know in advance the level of funding they can expect from Juneau."

Source: Palin-Parnell campaign booklet: *New Energy for Alaska.* November 3, 2006.

Supports charter schools, home schools, and other alternatives.

"My administration will support existing programs that already offer alternative school options available throughout the state, including charter schools, rural boarding schools, home school options, correspondence schools, vocational/technical, and magnet schools. There are many successes out there that we can look to as models. My administration will support and expand existing programs that successfully offer new approaches to ensure an appropriate education for every child in Alaska."

Source: Palin-Parnell campaign booklet: *New Energy for Alaska.* November 3, 2006.

Target early education programs to at-risk groups.

"The state should target early-education programs to specific at-risk groups that truly need them. These groups will benefit from access to high-quality programs currently out of their reach. We must find a way for these children to obtain a safe and positive environment in their early years. Today, social and economic pressures sometimes encourage both parents to return to work outside the home. My administration will publish useful educational material for parents about children in their early years."

Source: Palin-Parnell campaign booklet: *New Energy for Alaska.* November 3, 2006.

Alignment between parents, teachers, schools, and business.

Alignment is the unity of purpose which brings parents, children, teachers, public administration and businesses together towards a common goal of quality education. Alignment towards the common goal is built upon the values of respect for one another, our unique cultures and traditions, and our individual personal values. Here is how Alignment fits together:

• Parents understand the importance of their involvement with and their responsibility for their child's education.

• Children attend class ready to learn.

• Teachers are allowed to teach without distraction.

• Administrations sustain an environment where performance and options are valued.

• Business will help define the outcomes needed for employment.

• Parents are the first educators.

• Teachers are responsible for providing a rich classroom environment.

• Administration is responsible to their community for costs, safety, and choice.

Source: Palin-Parnell campaign booklet: *New Energy for Alaska.* November 3, 2006.

ENERGY AND OIL

Produce more of our own oil and gas for national security.

"The stakes for our nation could not be higher. When a hurricane strikes in the Gulf of Mexico, this country should not be so dependent on imported oil that we are forced to draw from our Strategic Petroleum Reserve. And families cannot throw away more and more of their paychecks on gas and heating oil.

"With Russia wanting to control a vital pipeline in the Caucasus, and to divide and intimidate our European allies by using energy as a weapon, we cannot leave ourselves at the mercy of foreign suppliers.

"To confront the threat that Iran might seek to cut off nearly a fifth of world energy supplies ... or that terrorists might strike again at the Abqaiq facility in Saudi Arabia ... or that Venezuela might shut off its oil deliveries ... we Americans need to produce more of our own oil and gas.

"And take it from a gal who knows the North Slope of Alaska: We've got lots of both."

Source: Speech at 2008 Republican National Convention, September 3, 2008.

Gas pipeline: history's largest private-sector infrastructure.

I fought to bring about the largest private-sector infrastructure project in North American history. And when that deal was struck, we began a nearly $40 billion natural gas pipeline to help lead America to energy independence. That pipeline, when the last section is laid and its valves are opened, will lead America one step farther away from dependence on dangerous foreign powers that do not have our interests at heart.

Source: Speech at 2008 Republican National Convention, September 3, 2008.

More pipelines; more nukes; more coal; more alternatives.

"Our opponents say, again and again, that drilling will not solve all of America's energy problems—as if we all didn't know that already. But the fact that drilling won't solve every problem is no excuse to do nothing at all.

"Starting in January, in a McCain-Palin Administration, we're going to lay more pipelines ... build more nuclear plants ... create jobs with clean coal ... and move forward on solar, wind, geothermal and other alternative sources."

Source: Speech at 2008 Republican National Convention, September 3, 2008.

Claimed major triumph: $500 million subsidy for gas pipeline.

Palin's intense pursuit of a pipeline to deliver natural gas from the North Slope of Alaska to market in the Lower 48 led to what her administration has claimed as a major triumph: the Legislature this summer approved her plan to give a $500 million subsidy to TransCanada, a Canadian company, to help build the project.

Rebuffing criticism of the pipeline subsidy, Ms. Palin has cast the pipeline as a way for Alaska to "end our dependence on foreign oil." She has said she hopes the pipeline effort will show that Alaska can contribute to a new energy economy, rather than be known as the state that receives more per capita federal spending than any other. Critics in the state complained that Palin undercut her clean-government image by appointing as her chief adviser on the pipeline a former lobbyist for TransCanada. The adviser, Marty Rutherford, her deputy commissioner of natural resources, earned about $40,000 lobbying the state government for a TransCanada subsidiary in 2003.

Source: *New York Times*, pp. A1 and A10, "An Outsider Who Charms," August 29, 2008.

Global warming affects Alaska, but is not man-made.

Q: What is your take on global warming and how is it affecting our country?

A: A changing environment will affect Alaska more than any other state because of our location. I'm not one, though, who would attribute it to being man-made.

Source: Q and A with Newsmax.com's Mike Coppock, August 29, 2008.

Resource rebate: suspend Alaska's eight-cent fuel tax for one year.

"I'm pleased to report to Alaskans that in early August, our Alaska Legislature agreed to approve a one-time resource rebate that returns part of our resource wealth to Alaskans—the owners in common of these resources. The rebate will be a direct payment of $1,200 to each Alaskan eligible for the 2008 Permanent Fund Dividend. The resource rebate was part of a larger energy package that also includes a 50 percent increase in the maximum loan amount for bulk fuel bridge and bulk fuel revolving loan funds to communities and cooperatives. Additionally, it suspends the state's 8-cent motor fuel tax on gasoline, marine fuel and aviation fuel for one year and strengthens the Power Cost Equalization Program.

"Our lawmakers also included an additional $60 million for the Home Energy Rebate Program operated by the Alaska Housing Finance Corporation and $50 million in grant funds to the Renewable Energy Fund, bringing the total available for renewable energy projects in FY 2009 to $100 million."

Source: Alaska Governor's Office: August 2008 Newsletter, August 20, 2008.

Gasline Inducement Act: 1,715-mile natural gas pipeline.

On August 1, the legislature awarded TC Alaska the AGIA license to move forward and build Alaska's natural gas pipeline. The Legislature also authorized my administration to award the Alaska Gasline Inducement Act license to TransCanada Alaska to initiate development of a 1,715-mile natural gas pipeline from Prudhoe Bay on the North Slope to the Alberta Hub in Canada. Lawmakers also appropriated $35.5 million for gas pipeline expenditures.

Source: Alaska Governor's Office: August 2008 Newsletter, August 20, 2008.

Commercialize Alaska's North Slope natural gas.

Governor Sarah Palin today signed Administrative Order 242, directing the state Department of Natural Resources and the Department of Revenue to work cooperatively with any organization or entity committed to commercializing Alaska's North Slope natural gas.

"This solidifies our commitment to facilitating an LNG project that is a product of market interest," Governor Palin said. "By committing both project capital and natural gas resources to a pipeline that would transport North Slope natural gas to tidewater, an LNG project can remain an integral element of the state's effort to deliver Alaska's gas to market."

Specifically, the Administrative Order instructs the two departments to provide specific kinds of support to those pursuing development of an economically and technically viable liquefied natural gas project. That support includes permitting coordination, fiscal and economic analysis, and facilitation of meetings with federal agencies.

Source: Alaska Governor's Office: press release, "Admin. Order 242," August 20, 2008.

Served as Alaska Oil and Gas Commissioner.

"[After serving as mayor], I was appointed as Oil and Gas Commissioner in the State of Alaska, on the Alaska Oil and Gas Conservation Commission, had decided that there were changes, positive changes, that had to be ushered into our state government, decided to run for governor and did so, was successful, and here we are."

Source: Q and A with *Time* magazine's Jay Newton Small Aug 14, 2008

Windfall oil profits tax prevents investment.

Palin [supported Obama's energy proposal but] questioned the means to pay for Obama's proposed rebate—a windfall profits tax on oil companies. In Alaska, the state's resource valuation system, ACES, provides strong incentives for companies to re-invest their profits in new production.

"Windfall profits taxes alone prevent additional investment in domestic production. Without new supplies from American reserves, our dependency and addiction to foreign sources of oil will continue," Palin said.

Source: Alaska Governor's Office: press release, "Obama Energy Plan," August 4, 2008.

Exxon-Mobil should pay $507 million for Exxon-Valdez spill.

Governor Palin today encouraged Exxon Mobil to pay the $507 million in punitive damages plus interest awarded by the U.S. Supreme Court to 32,000 plaintiffs in the 1989 Exxon-Valdez oil-spill lawsuit. "These people have suffered long enough," Governor Palin said. "While Exxon may have the ability to delay payments, I strongly encourage them to bring this sad chapter in our history to a long-overdue conclusion. It is time to end the misery so everyone can move on."

The governor is hopeful plaintiffs will receive payments this fall. So far, though, Exxon has not indicated whether it will cut checks to plaintiffs right away, or seek further reductions in the award as the case goes back to the lower courts.

Source: Alaska Governor's Office: Press release 08-106, "Exxon," July 1, 2008.

Unlock Arctic National Wildlife Refuge (ANWR)

Q: The governor of Alaska sent a letter to Senate Leader Harry Reid with a very clear demand—drill in ANWR now. Governor Sarah Palin is on the phone right now. Governor, I'm curious how you were received today, when so many of your constituents, I would assume, want to protect the land, not drill. How did it go today?

A: I'll correct you there with all due respect—the people of Alaska understand that Alaska has so much to contribute in terms of energy sources to the rest of the U.S. Folks up here want ANWR to be unlocked by the federal government so that we can drill. We've got a tremendous amount of resources up here, and we're ready, willing and able to contribute. I think Washington doesn't understand that we're at a real critical crossroads: We are either going to become more and more dependent on foreign sources of energy, or we're going to be able to secure our nation and drill domestically for safe, stable, clean supplies of energy that we have here. We have them in Alaska.

Source: Fox News Channel "Your World" with Neil Cavuto, June 27, 2008.

Energy relief plan: $100 per person monthly for oil and gas.

Returning surplus funds through grants to electric utilities will result in a 60-percent reduction for all ratepayers. The benefit will flow to homeowners, renters, schools, governments, and businesses.

In addition, there will be conservation incentives for the utilities. For every one-percent reduction in 2008 kilowatt-hour sales from 2007 sales, the state will make a year-end contribution for capital energy projects to the utility.

The Energy Debit Card will go out to every qualifying [Alaska resident]. The benefit will be $100 per month per recipient. The temporary Energy Debit Card can be used for purchases from Alaska energy vendors, such as heating oil distributors, natural gas utilities, electric utilities, gas stations, and other retail fueling stations.

The value of this plan is approximately $1.2 billion. The grant to electric utilities is expected to be $475 million, while the Energy Debit Card totals are forecast to be $729 million. The governor has proposed this energy relief plan for one year.

Source: Alaska Governor's Office: Press release 08-074 "Energy Plan," May 15, 2008.

Drill in ANWR

Governor Sarah Palin released the following statement after President Bush renewed his call to open the Arctic National Wildlife Refuge for oil exploration in the face of surging gasoline prices: "President Bush is right. Across the nation, communities are feeling the pinch of high energy costs. It is absurd that we are borrowing from one foreign country to buy oil from another. It is a threat to our national security and economic well-being. It is well past time for America to develop our own supplies."

Source: Alaska Governor's Office: Press release 8-068, "ANWR," April 29, 2008.

Fully fund the Petroleum Systems Integrity Office

Governor Sarah Palin today strongly urged lawmakers to restore critical funding for the Petroleum Systems Integrity Office (PSIO), which exercises oversight of the maintenance of facilities, equipment, and infrastructure for sustained production and transportation of oil and natural gas resources in Alaska.

"I'm disappointed that house finance subcommittee members removed $523,000 in funding for PSIO from my budget. Facing the prospect of the largest construction project in North America, a natural gas pipeline, we must demonstrate to Alaskans and the nation that we provide sound oversight of the systems that are needed to develop our resources. I am hopeful the full finance committee will restore funding for critical PSIO positions needed to accomplish this mission."

The money would fund personnel for investigation of system-integrity breaches and implementation of a statewide quality-assurance program.

Source: Alaska Governor's Office: press release, "Funding Restored," February 25, 2008.

$250M for proven alternative energy, including wind and hydroelectric power.

"We need a comprehensive approach to long-term energy plans, not just fiscal 'shots-in-the-arm.' I'm appointing an Energy Coordinator, to activate a statewide energy plan. We'll use earnings from a $250-million 'Renewable Energy Fund' for alternative projects, like hydro, wind, geothermal, and biomass. These projects cannot even flirt with snake-oil science— they will be real, doable, and economic. Alaska's plan can lead America toward energy security and a cleaner, safer world."

Source: State of the State Address to the 25th Alaska
Legislature, January 15, 2008.

Gas pipelines are approved if they meet Alaska's needs.

"An example of our self-determination is our natural gas pipeline vehicle: the Alaska Gasline Inducement Act. AGIA's competitive process is built on Alaska's 'must-haves.' Finally we will have an 'open access' gas line so new explorers can produce new reserves, providing in-state use of our gas and careers for Alaskans. Without AGIA's requirements, we'd be leveraged by a small group of companies. We can't surrender revenue, judicial process, and our sovereignty. A respected pipeline construction company, TransCanada, submitted a proposal that meets all of Alaska's requirements. AGIA cleared the path for our gas to feed hungry local markets and to help secure the country with a safe, stable, and domestic supply of clean energy. An AGIA license gets the ball rolling on our terms—and opens the door to innovative and strategic partnerships. We are reasonable and open to those partnerships that, at the end of the day, will get that long-awaited gas line built."

Source: State of the State Address to the 25th Alaska
Legislature, January 15, 2008.

National energy policy essential.

Governor Palin yesterday sent a letter to senators and the Bush Administration advocating defeat of a bill that would prohibit oil and natural gas development in the Arctic National Wildlife Refuge.

The legislation, sponsored by Sen. Joe Leiberman (I-CT), aims to designate ANWR as a wilderness. Palin criticized the bill as it would effectively ban oil and gas exploration in the most promising unexplored regions in North America—the coastal plain of ANWR. In the letter, Governor Palin states that national energy policy must include a variety of resources:

"I don't see national energy policy as an either/or proposition," said Governor Palin. "Rather, we need to develop secure domestic sources of conventional energy, such as oil and natural gas, while also researching and developing alternative and renewable energy."

Governor Palin reminded senators that opening ANWR to oil and gas exploration would reduce U.S. dependence on foreign sources of oil, increase federal revenues, and create hundreds of thousands of jobs.

Source: Letter to members of the U.S. Senate and Pres. Bush, November 10, 2007.

Fund cellulosic biofuel research in Farm Bill.

We urge you to allocate the maximum feasible level of funding for the programs in Title IX in the 2007 Farm Bill. If the nation is to pursue energy independence, we must look beyond traditional biofuels production. Governors urge Congress to include a strong energy title as part of the Farm Bill that provides technical and financial assistance to expand the use of farm and forest biomass for renewable energy production.

Local production of renewable biomass energy benefits the national economy, promotes national and regional energy security and stimulates the rural economy through the creation of high quality jobs. Encouraging such production will require increased federal investment in programs that support cellulosic biofuels research, increased biodiesel production and use, increases in wind and solar energy and energy from animal wastes, improvements in energy efficiency, bio-based product development, effective carbon storage, and other renewable technologies.

Source: Letter from two governors to Senate Committee on Agriculture, October 30, 2007.

Submitted legislation to build natural AGIA gas pipeline.

Governor Palin submitted the Alaska Gasline Inducement Act (AGIA) to the legislature on her 89th day in office. The legislation will act as a vehicle to get a natural gas pipeline built and bring the state's substantial gas reserves to market. The AGIA offers a number of inducements for those who hold gas leases and for those who want to build the line. In return, the state will provide a matching capital contribution and insist on the state's must-haves: project benchmarks, gas for Alaskans, expansion capabilities, and jobs for Alaskans. The state is committed to ensuring that Alaskans will be trained and ready to build the gas line. Governor Palin recently traveled to Washington, D.C., where she received encouragement for the AGIA from

Alaska's Congressional Delegation, FERC officials and members of the Bush Administration.

Source: Alaska Governor's Office: press release, "100th Day," March 13, 2007.

Stranded Gas Development Act no longer applies.

"My administration will pursue the gas line plan that is best for ALL Alaskans. How do we get there? Through a two-step process. First, we acknowledge that the Stranded Gas Development Act (SGDA), under which the previous administration negotiated with the 'Big Three' producers (ExxonMobil, ConocoPhillips, and BP), no longer applies. The legislature's own experts have testified that the gas can no longer be deemed 'stranded' due to long-term economic conditions."

Source: Campaign website, www.palinforgovernor.com, "Issues," November 7, 2006.

Open ANWR.

"I believe in protecting Alaska's environment through fair enforcement of our environmental laws. Having a clean record on environmental regulation is critical to getting ANWR open and maintaining our fisheries mining, timber, and tourism industries. I would also revisit the change in regulations on the Alaska Coastal Zone Management program in which the past administration by eliminating the rights of local districts to write specific local enforceable policies on important issues like subsistence."

Source: Campaign website, www.palinforgovernor.com, "Issues," November 7, 2006.

Chaired the Alaska Oil and Gas Conservation Commission.

• Sarah is the one with experience and energy to move Alaska forward!

• Sarah Palin will use her experience as Chairman of the Alaska Oil and Gas Conservation Commission to negotiate a fair gas pipeline agreement that puts Alaska first and creates jobs for all Alaskans.

Source: Palin-Parnell campaign booklet: *New Energy for Alaska.* November 3, 2006.

Pursue gas line plan that is best for all Alaskans.

"My administration will pursue the gas line plan that is best for ALL Alaskans. All qualified and viable proposals and applicants will be considered. How do we get there? First, we acknowledge that the Stranded Gas Development Act (SGDA) no longer applies. The producers want to amend the SGDA to fit their proposed contract within the technical confines of that law. However, the legislature's own experts have testified that the gas can no longer be deemed 'stranded' due to long-term economic conditions."

Source: Palin-Parnell campaign booklet: *New Energy for Alaska.* November 3, 2006.

Met with producers and employee groups for pipeline deal.

Q: Will you limit your negotiations on the gas pipeline to the producers or will you reopen discussions with others?

KNOWLES: I would look to all of the proposals to see what is the best deal for Alaska. The next governor is going to have to sit down with Alaska business leaders, members of the oil and gas industry and others to negotiate an Alaska gas line on Alaska's terms. Sarah has refused to meet with the executives and employees of ConocoPhillips, BP, Alyeska, with the regional CEOs of the Native corporations. I believe that we cannot afford to have a governor who is AWOL. You cannot delegate leadership.

PALIN: That is an untruthful statement. I've met with Exxon. I've met with ConocoPhillips. I've met with the BP employee group and the ConocoPhillips folks. Heck, I have the endorsement of the North Slope union hands up there.

Source: Alaska 2006 Governor Debate at Anchorage Rotary, October 31, 2006.

Firm start date as part of gas line incentive offer.

Q: Do you believe the state should demand a firm construction start date for a gas line, despite the uncertainties of construction costs, permits, and financing?

A: Yes. If the state is going to offer incentives—and award them to a specific proposal—it is reasonable to expect a firm start date. Otherwise, other proposals need to be given the opportunity to begin construction.

Source: *Anchorage Daily News*: 2006 gubernatorial candidate profile, October 22, 2006.

Opposes natural gas reserves tax—it's not earned income yet.

Q: Do you support the natural gas reserves tax on the November 7 ballot? If it passed, how would that affect your negotiations with the producers on a gas pipeline?

A: I am opposed. This initiative is akin to taxing income before it is even earned. The way to get an agreement on building a pipeline is to negotiate, not litigate.

Q: Do you support the Petroleum Profits Tax passed by the legislature and signed into law by Governor Murkowski? If no, why not?

A: My preference was a tax on the gross price with a price-progressive index. We need to see how companies apply the tax credits within the law. If the credits are abused and Alaska is shortchanged, changes will be proposed. The intent of the credits is to encourage new exploration and infrastructure development.

Source: *Anchorage Daily News*: 2006 gubernatorial candidate profile, October 22, 2006.

Analyze potential costs associated with climate change.

Q: What role does state government have, if any, in addressing global warming and climate change?

A: We need to analyze the potential economic costs, needs and opportunities associated with climate change. Let's be cautious in how we react—to make sure we don't overreact. The Alaska Climate Impact Assessment Commission is supposed to assess the situation and issue a report on March 1, 2007. This is a good start.

Source: *Anchorage Daily News*: 2006 gubernatorial candidate profile, October 22, 2006.

ENVIRONMENT

Opposed protections for salmon from mining contamination.

This month, Ms. Palin issued a last-minute statement of opposition to a ballot measure that would have provided added protections for salmon from potential contamination from mining, an action seen as crucial to its defeat.

Source: *New York Times*, pp. A1 & A10, "An Outsider Who Charms," August 29, 2008.

Sue U.S. government to stop listing the polar bear as an endangered species.

Governor Sarah Palin announced today the State of Alaska has filed a lawsuit in U.S. District Court for the District of Columbia seeking to overturn Interior

Secretary Dirk Kempthorne's decision to list the polar bear as threatened under the Endangered Species Act.

This action follows written notice given more than 60 days ago, asking that the regulation listing the polar bear as threatened be withdrawn. "We believe that the Service's decision to list the polar bear was not based on the best scientific and commercial data available," Governor Palin said.

The service's analysis failed to adequately consider the polar bear's survival through prior warming periods, and its findings that the polar bear is threatened by sea-ice habitat loss are not warranted. The service also failed to adequately consider the existing regulatory mechanisms which have resulted in a sustainable, worldwide polar bear population that has more than doubled in number over the last 40 years to 20,000-25,000 bears.

Source: Alaska Governor's Office: press release, "Polar Bear," August 4, 2008.

We must encourage timber, mining, drilling, and fishing.

"Industry knows we want responsible development. Anadarko will drill Alaska's first-ever gas-targeted wells on the North Slope. Chevron, FEX, Renaissance—many others are exploring. That's ratification of AGIA's promise to make investments profitable for industrious explorers. There's more we can do to ramp up development. Our new reservoir study can increase development and we will ensure better, publicly supported project coordination. To cultivate timber and agriculture, we're encouraging responsible economic efforts to revitalize our once-robust industries. We can and must continue to develop our economy, because we cannot and must not rely so heavily on federal government earmarks."

Source: State of the State Address to the 25th Alaska Legislature, January 15, 2008.

Wolf predator control.

Governor Palin criticized Congressman George Miller's (D-CA) legislation to eliminate an important element of wildlife management by the State of Alaska. "Moose & caribou are important food for Alaskans, and Representative Miller's bill threatens that food supply," said Governor Palin. "Representative Miller doesn't understand rural Alaska, doesn't comprehend wildlife management in the North, and doesn't appreciate the Tenth Amendment that gives states the right to manage their own affairs."

Miller's bill would ban the shooting of wolves from aircraft, a component of moose and caribou management plans in five specific areas of Alaska. Contrary to what Representative Miller said in Washington yesterday, there is no "aerial hunting" of wolves in Alaska, Palin said. "Our science-driven and abundance-based predator management program involves volunteers who are permitted to use aircraft to kill some predators where we are trying to increase opportunities for Alaskans to put healthy food on their families' dinner tables. It is not hunting."

Source: Alaska Governor's Office: Press release 07-197, "Wildlife," September 26, 2007.

Beluga whales are not endangered.

Governor Palin has told the federal government that the state is extremely concerned about a proposal to list Cook Inlet beluga whales as an endangered species, and urged the National Marine Fisheries Service (NMFS) not to list the species.

"Our scientists feel confident that it would be unwarranted to list Cook Inlet belugas now," Governor Palin said. "Seven years ago, NMFS determined that these whales weren't endangered, and since then, we've actually seen the beginnings of an increase in their population. We are all doing everything we can to help protect these important marine mammals."

The state submitted 95 pages of data and formal comments to NMFS on the proposed listing, pointing out that the Cook Inlet stock of belugas is recovering from an "unsustainable harvest" in the early 1990s. "I am especially concerned that an unnecessary federal listing and designation of critical habitat would do serious long-term damage to the vibrant economy of the Cook Inlet area," Palin said.

Source: Alaska Governor's Office: Press release 07-175, "Beluga," August 7, 2007.

Provide stability in regulations for developers.

"I'm keenly aware of sharply declining production from North Slope fields. The amount of oil currently flowing through the pipeline is less than half of what it was at its peak. We must look to responsible development throughout the state—from the Slope all the way down to the Southeast—every region participating! From further oil and gas development to fishing, mining, timber, and tourism, these developments remain the core of our state. We provide stability in regulations for our developers."

Source: State of the State Address to the 24th Alaska Legislature, January 17, 2007.

Convince the rest of the nation to open ANWR.

"The standard should be no different for industry. Ironically, we're trying to convince the rest of the nation to open ANWR, but we can't even get our own Point Thomson, which is right on the edge of ANWR, developed! We are ready for that gas to be tapped so we can fill a natural-gas pipeline. I promise to vigorously defend Alaska's rights, as resource owners, to develop and receive appropriate value for our resources."

Source: State of the State Address to the 24th Alaska Legislature, January 17, 2007.

Fish platform: "Resource First" philosophy

Fish Platform: Do What's Right For Alaska's Fishing Communities

- "Resource First" Philosophy
- Professional ADF&G Management with Adequate Funding
- Fishery Advisor

- Balanced Board and Council Appointments
- Aggressive Marketing Campaign
- No Fish Farming

"I am not only a champion for Alaska's fishing industry, but a part of it. My family is proud to be a Bristol Bay fishing family. If we manage for abundance, we should have enough fish for all our needs."

Source: Palin-Parnell campaign booklet: *New Energy for Alaska.* November 3, 2006.

Rail provides critical link for business development.

- The railroad provides a critical link to interior Alaska for hauling equipment and materials, as well as passengers.
- Rail service and use has improved greatly over the past few years. The system is being managed, maintained, and upgraded to better standards.
- Rail development is ideal for transport of heavy items. If it is economically beneficial over the long term, railways should be utilized to open up those areas of Alaska currently not served by roads in order to support business development.

Source: Palin-Parnell campaign booklet: *New Energy for Alaska.* November 3, 2006.

Supports "Roads to Resources."

When it comes to spending state money, Palin is generally conservative. Yet Palin supports the state's "roads to resources program," which funds roads to mines and other natural-resources projects, such as oil and gas. Knowles say the state should not subsidize road construction to new mines.

Source: *Anchorage Daily News*: 2006 gubernatorial candidate profile, October 31, 2006.

Don't duplicate effort in monitoring cruise-ship emissions.

Palin questioned environmental aspects of the new cruise-ship law in an October 17 letter to the Alaska Travel Industry Association, the state's major tourism group. Palin questioned whether the new environmental monitoring is "redundant" under state law and she said no other Alaska business faces the consumer disclosures now required for cruise lines. Palin worried about the law's environmental enforcement and its requirement for cruise lines to disclose their commissions for channeling passengers to sight-seeing companies, rafting businesses, gift shops, and other on-shore vendors.

The state Department of Environmental Conservation and state Department of Revenue are now writing the regulations to enforce the taxes, environmental permits, and disclosure rules. The new taxes and rules go into effect December 17.

Source: *Anchorage Daily News*: 2006 gubernatorial candidate profile, October 30, 2006.

Don't amend Alaska's constitution for rural subsistence fishing.

Subsistence fishing might be the issue that most clearly separates Knowles and Palin. 83 percent of rural households have subsistence fishing permits. Knowles expended much effort as governor trying to reconcile state and federal law, the latter of which gives rural residents priority to fish and game on the vast federal lands in Alaska. He wants an amendment to the Alaska Constitution to cement the rural priority. Pundits reckon that position is a plus for Knowles among rural voters.

Palin opposes a constitutional amendment, saying equality provisions should not be tampered with. She says the state should work toward another resolution that protects subsistence for those who need it most.

Knowles and Palin are in accord on one final item: No fish farms in Alaska waters.

Source: *Anchorage Daily News*: 2006 gubernatorial candidate profile, October 29, 2006.

FAMILIES AND CHILDREN

Special-needs children will have her as a friend and advocate.

"Sometimes even the greatest joys bring challenge. In April, my husband and I welcomed our littlest one into the world, a perfectly beautiful baby boy named Trig [who has Down's Syndrome].

"Children with special needs inspire a special love. To the families of special-needs children all across this country, I have a message: For years, you sought to make America a more welcoming place for your sons and daughters. I pledge to you that if we are elected, you will have a friend and advocate in the White House."

Source: Speech at 2008 Republican National Convention, September 3, 2008.

Recognizes the vital role of family child care homes.

- WHEREAS, family child care provides a vital service for Alaska families, neighborhoods, and communities. By caring for the youngest Alaskans in home-based environments, family child care providers ensure that children are able to grow and learn where they are also happy, safe, secure, and stimulated.
- WHEREAS, family child care providers understand the importance of family and home; ensure long-term stability; and give parents convenient support close to home, among other benefits.
- WHEREAS, family child care is thus able to nurture children across a broad spectrum of development. With help from neighborhoods and communities, they can uniquely cater to, support, and include children of all levels of ability, need, activity, and curiosity.
- Family Child Care Week in Alaska, and encourage all Alaskans to recognize the vital role family child care homes play in the lives of our children.

Source: Alaska Governor's Office: Proclamation, "Child Care," March 28, 2008.

Opposes explicit sex-education programs.

Q: Will you support funding for abstinence-until-marriage education instead of for explicit sex-education programs, school-based clinics, and the distribution of contraceptives in schools?

A: Yes, the explicit sex-ed programs will not find my support.

Source: Eagle Forum 2006 Gubernatorial Candidate Questionnaire, July 31, 2006.

FOREIGN POLICY

Peace Corps strengthens US ties abroad and enriches US at home.

- The Peace Corps has become an enduring symbol of our nation's commitment to encourage progress, create opportunity, and expand development at the grass-roots level in the developing world.

- More than 187,000 Americans have served as Peace Corps volunteers in 139 countries since 1961 [including] 837 men and women from the State of Alaska.

- Peace Corps volunteers have strengthened the ties of friendship and understanding among the people of the US and those of other countries.

- Peace Corp volunteers, enriched by their experiences overseas, have brought to their communities throughout the US, a deeper understanding of other cultures and traditions, thereby bringing a domestic dividend to our nation.

• NOW, THEREFORE, I, Sarah Palin, Governor of the State of Alaska, do hereby proclaim February 26-March 4, 2007, as Peace Corps Week in Alaska and encourage all Alaskans to recognize the achievements of the Peace Corps.

Source: Alaska Governor's Office: Proclamation, "Peace Corps," January 29, 2007.

FREE TRADE

Trade important to Alaska.

Alaskans have been first-rate at international trade for decades. To our friends in international markets, thank you for your friendship and trade. Alaska welcomes your business and investment.

International trade is important to Alaska. Our exports grew more than 12 percent last year, and, for the first time, our annual exports topped $4 billion in 2006. We are helping our economy and economies around the world through trade.

In all our efforts, we will keep Alaska residents first. We will help Alaska businesses succeed in their key international markets. We will improve Alaska's positive international relations with our key trading partners. We will help open new doors.

Education helps trade, too. International courses at our schools and universities help us excel in international markets. We must further prepare Alaskans for international investment and trade opportunities by encouraging education that includes strong workforce development for our high-wage energy and mining industries.

Source: Letter from the governor on state trade website, September 1, 2008.

Allow wineries to ship by mail within state.

Governor Sarah Palin signed into law today House Bill 34, which allows the holder of a winery license to ship up to five gallons of wine within Alaska. The new law will help small Alaska wineries compete with out-of-state wineries through mail, fax orders, and Internet sales, provided that the shipping address is not located in an area that has prohibited importation of alcohol. Before today, Alaskans could order wine from outside Alaska, but they could not order from in-state wineries.

Source: Alaska Governor's Office: Press release 07-138, "Wineries," June 5, 2008.

International markets and companies trust Alaska.

International markets and companies trust Alaska's stable, transparent business climate. They appreciate the creativity and friendliness they find in our state. I want to honor Alaskans who connect us all to the world. The North Star Awards are a good way to celebrate the international know-how of Alaskans.

Source: Statement to Announce the North Star Awards, April 2, 2008.

Exempt Alaskan cruise ships from customs rule changes.

Governor Sarah Palin has asked the U.S. Bureau of Customs and Border Protection to back off on a proposed rule interpretation that would harm the Alaska tourism industry. At issue is the agency's proposed interpretation of an 1886 maritime law that would require foreign-owned cruise ships running between the US West Coast and Hawaii to spend at least 48 hours in a foreign port. The vessels would also have to spend at least half as much time in a foreign port as spent in all US ports of call.

If applied to Alaska cruises, the new interpretation would force cruise lines to significantly cut back their time in Alaska ports, pulling hundreds of millions of dollars a year out of the Alaska economy.

"The proposed rule interpretation, aimed at Hawaiian Coastwise Cruises, would be a dramatic and abrupt shift in policy," Governor Palin said in a letter to the bureau. "Taking something that is working well and changing it—much less on 30 days notice—is not reasonable public policy."

Source: Alaska Governor's Office: Press release 07-246, "Cruises," December 26, 2007.

GOVERNMENT REFORM

Comprehensive ethics reform: change politics as usual.

Governor Palin today signed House Bill 109 into law. The legislation improves Alaska's ethics and disclosure laws. "It was so gratifying to be a part of a bipartisan effort, where the focus was on doing the right thing for the people of Alaska," said Governor Palin. "Comprehensive ethics reform was a priority of mine. HB 109 is a good first step toward changing the culture of politics as usual."

- House Bill 109 … Requiring ethics training for lobbyists and their employers
  - Increasing restrictions on lobbyists' gifts
  - Barring persons with certain felony convictions from lobbying
  - Barring spouses and domestic partners of legislators from lobbying for pay
  - Prohibiting certain high-level executive branch officials from lobbying for one year after leaving those positions.
  - Requiring electronic filing of campaign and financial disclosures
  - Prohibits agreements to exchange campaign contributions to elected officials or candidates for changing their votes or positions on a matter

Source: Alaska Governor's Office: Press release 07-162 "Ethics Bill," July 9, 2007.

Presented comprehensive ethics bill in early 2007.

Keeping her campaign promise to govern in an open and transparent fashion, Governor Palin presented an ethics bill to the legislature on January 24. The comprehensive bill tightens ethics within the executive branch, but touches upon all public servants. The bill mandates more detail in financial disclosure, encourages electronic access, further defines conflicts of interest, bans gifts from lobbyists, and tightens certain employment restrictions after leaving office.

Source: Alaska Governor's Office: press release, "100th Day," March 13, 2007.

Sold previous governor's jet.

Governor Sarah Palin today [decided] to sell the jet that was purchased by former Governor Frank Murkowski's administration. The Westwind II will be put up for auction on eBay. "The purchase of the jet was impractical and unwise and it's time to get rid of it," said Governor Palin. "In the meantime, I am keeping my promise not to set foot on the jet."

The state has successfully used eBay in the past to sell state assets, including a former Marine Highways ferry, and several public safety aircraft. The state's surplus property disposal policy is to use eBay for high-value, mobile assets because it offers the widest possible exposure for these types of sales at a low cost.

The jet was purchased for $2,692,600 in November 2005 by the Murkowski Administration. Until final sale, Governor Palin has authorized the Department of Public Safety to use the jet for suitable operational purposes.

Source: Alaska Governor's Office: Press release 06-006A, "E-Bay." December 12, 2006.

Attended numerous debates and did not avoid any unnecessarily.

"[With regards to the previous BP debate]: What I did out there in Wasilla, also, I was able to apply those Rotarian values, that four-way test about truthfulness and fairness. And I wish that that applied to state politics and to campaigns. Just yesterday, a real quick example of how the nature of the beast of politics is so far from that four-way test of Rotarians, it's so unfortunate.

"Yesterday—at the BP forum—I was invited weeks ago to show up. Well, I'd already met with the BP group. I just met with the president of BP. Wasn't able to re-arrange my schedule to get there yesterday. And I get home last night and all over the news is: 'Sarah was a no-show. She wasn't at the debate.' There's a sign out front making it look like I was supposed to be there and I wasn't. But I wasn't supposed to be there."

Source: Alaska 2006 Governor Debate: at Anchorage Rotary, October 31, 2006.

Supports state funding for Gravina Island bridge.

Q: Would you continue state funding for the proposed Knik Arm and Gravina Island bridges? [Note: The Gravina Island bridge later became known as the "Bridge to Nowhere."]

A: Yes. I would like to see Alaska's infrastructure projects built sooner rather than later. The window is now—while our congressional delegation is in a strong position to assist.

Source: *Anchorage Daily News*: 2006 gubernatorial candidate profile, October 22, 2006.

GUN CONTROL

Hunts and fishes.

Her father shot the grizzly bear whose hide is now draped over the sofa in her office. She, too, hunts and fishes. She runs marathons. She delivered her fifth child during her first term as governor. They call her husband, the reigning champion in the annual Iron Dog snowmachine race, First Dude.

Though indisputably Alaskan, she rose to prominence by bucking the state's rigid Republican hierarchy, impressing voters more with gumption, warmth and charm than an established record in government.

Source: *New York Times*, pp. A1 & A10, "An Outsider Who Charms," August 29, 2008.

Supports ending D.C.'s 32-year-old ban on handguns.

Governor Sarah Palin today lauded the U.S. Supreme Court's landmark decision upholding the right of Americans to own guns for self-defense, hunting and other purposes. The high court's 5-4 ruling in District of Columbia vs. Heller affirmed gun rights by striking down the District's 32-year-old ban on handguns.

"This decision is a victory for all Alaskans and individual Americans. The right to own guns and use them responsibly is something I and many other Alaskans cherish," Governor Palin said. "I applaud the court for standing up for the constitution and the right of Americans to keep and bear arms."

The State of Alaska in February joined a multi-state *amicus brief* written by the State of Texas in support of the Second Amendment right of individual Americans to bear arms.

Source: Alaska Governor's Office: press release, "2nd Amendment," June 26, 2008.

Lifelong NRA member and champion of right to bear arms.

Governor Sarah Palin announced the State of Alaska will join the multi-state *amicus brief* authored by the State of Texas in support of the Second Amendment right of individual Americans to bear arms. The Texas *amicus brief* in the case of Washington, D.C. v. Heller will be filed by February 11, 2008.

Governor Palin, a lifelong member of the National Rifle Association, has long been a champion of the constitutional right to bear arms, as well as a proponent of gun safety programs for Alaska's youth.

"I am proud to join the State of Texas in support of the Second Amendment," Governor Palin said. "We need to send a strong message that law-abiding citizens have a right to own firearms for personal protection, for hunting, and for any other lawful purpose."

Source: Alaska Governor's Office: press release, "2nd Amendment," February 8, 2008.

Supports Constitutional right to bear arms.

"I am a lifetime member of the NRA, I support our constitutional right to bear arms, and I am a proponent of gun safety programs for Alaska's youth."

Source: Campaign website, www.palinforgovernor.com, "Issues," November 7, 2006.

HEALTH CARE

Supports Organ Donor program.

Governor Palin today applauded the milestone that more than half of Alaska residents—335,033 people—have signed up to be organ and tissue donors. Alaska is the first state with a donor registry to enroll more than half of its state's population. The Governor, First Gentleman, and their two oldest children are organ and tissue donors.

"I am proud that so many residents recognize the life-giving benefits of organ and tissue donation," Governor Palin said. "Their willingness to donate demonstrates the selfless and generous nature of Alaskans."

April is National Donate Life Month. Every day in April, people across the U.S. make a special effort to celebrate the tremendous generosity of those who have saved lives by becoming organ, tissue, marrow, and blood donors. Life Alaska Donor Services is the tissue donation organization serving the State of Alaska, offering the option of donation to families who have suffered a death.

Source: Alaska Governor's Office: Press release 08-057 "Organ Donor," April 11, 2008.

Health care must be market-and-business driven.

Governor Sarah Palin today introduced the Alaska Health Care Transparency Act which will provide more effective tools to help Alaskans access affordable health care, and to ensure that our health care system is responsive to changing demographics and market conditions.

The bill would establish an Alaska Health Care Information Office to give consumers factual information on quality, costs, and other important matters to help them make better-informed decisions about health care in the state. Recognizing that health care must be market-and business-driven, rather than restricted by government, Governor Palin is proposing a repeal of the Certificate of Need program (CON). CON is a regulatory process that requires certain health care providers to obtain state approval before offering certain new or expanded services. [Palin's administration] concluded that the CON program does not benefit the citizens of Alaska, given the litigious environment surrounding it.

Source: Alaska Governor's Office: press release, "Transparency," January 19, 2008.

Health is a personal responsibility.

"Our choices often lead to heart disease, diabetes, underage drinking, drugs, violence, and abuse. Soaring health and public safety costs are sometimes unfairly passed on to others. But more importantly, by ignoring or accepting selfish choices that cause the abuse, children, families and entire communities are destroyed. Government cannot cure all ills. And don't assume more laws foisted on Alaskans are the only answer—most 'bad activity' is already illegal. We have got to make wise, healthy personal choices, including choosing not to ignore child abuse. I'm counting on families, communities and faith-based groups to step up together to help passionately here, too."

Source: State of the State Address to the 25th Alaska Legislature, January 15, 2008.

"Together, let's provide the services that our constitution requires, constitutional services such as education, public safety, and a solid infrastructure—and let's do them right. Let's commit to take responsibility for good stewardship when we're developing our natural resources. Let's remember that Alaskans are capable and they are created to work. So when government provides education and job training, every able-bodied Alaskan is expected to work and not simply rely on the government to provide. Let's take personal responsibility in all areas of life—including health. What we consume and engage in impacts not just our personal health, but our communities, too.

"Let's reign in government growth so individual liberty and opportunity can expand. And let's expect that every region contributes to our economy, to fulfill our promise to be a self-sufficient state made up of the hardest-working, most grateful Americans in our nation."

Source: State of the State Address to the 25th Alaska Legislature, January 15, 2008.

Doctors, not bureaucracies, should manage health care.

"I established our Health Care Strategies Council, and we'll pursue many of their recommendations, starting with our Health Care Transparency Act, requiring that consumers get better information about prices and quality of their own care. We will allow competition. Under our present Certificate of Need (CON) process, costs and needs don't drive health care choices—bureaucracy does! Our system is broken and expensive. We propose, as many states have, eliminating the CON, to increase choice and to manage rising costs. Currently nine CON lawsuits are adversely affecting consumers. Alaskans want health care in the hands of doctors, not lobbyists and lawyers. We are considering what other fiscally conservative states have done to incentivize employers to provide medical insurance for employees, based on the free market."

Source: State of the State Address to the 25th Alaska Legislature, January 15, 2008.

Flexibility in government regulations to allow competition.

"I look forward to working with affected parties to find the necessary solutions that will lead to more affordable health care for Alaskans. I support flexibility in government regulations that allow competition in health care that is needed, and is proven to be good for the consumer, which will drive down health-care costs and reduce the need for government subsidies. I also support patients in their rightful demands to have access to full medical billing information."

Source: Campaign website, www.palinforgovernor.com, "Issues," November 7, 2006.

More affordable health care via competition.

"Obviously, high medical costs are hurting Alaskans and our Medicaid budget has quadrupled in the past 10 years. Solutions to this problem are complex, and no one person has all the answers. I look forward to working with affected parties to find the necessary solutions that will lead to more affordable health care for Alaskans. I support flexibility in government regulations that allow competition in health care that is needed, and is proven to be good for the consumer, which will drive down health-care costs and reduce the need for government subsidies. I also support patients in their rightful demands to have access to full medical billing information."

Source: Palin-Parnell campaign booklet: *New Energy for Alaska.* November 3, 2006.

HOMELAND SECURITY

Strong military and sound energy.

Q: If you were running for president, what causes would you champion?

A: I would push for a strong military and a sound energy policy. I believe that Alaska can help set an example on energy policy.

Source: Q &A with Newsmax.com's Mike Coppock, August 29, 2008.

Armed forces, including my son, give us security and freedom.

"Let us pay tribute to all our men and women in uniform, and their families, and those who've previously served our great nation. Their fight for freedom allows us to assemble tonight—with liberty and security! Because of their sacrifices we are free to do our jobs here. And we thank them. Todd and our son Track who is proudly serving in the U.S. Army, thank you [all] for your service."

Source: State of the State Address to the 25th Alaska Legislature, January 15, 2008.

Ask all candidates, "Are you doing all you can for security?"

Q: Your views on national security issues?

A: I think candidates are going to be asked, are you doing—and are your intentions to do—all that you can to help secure these United States? And I think every elected official needs to ask themselves that. And I say that, even personally. My one and only son, my 18-year-old, he just signed up for the United States Army. He is at boot camp right now and I'm thinking, you know, this kid is doing all that he can within his power to help secure and defend the United States. Every elected official had better be asking themselves, are you doing as much also? Are you doing all that you can?

Source: Interview with Charlie Rose, October 12, 2007.

Visits Kuwait; encourages Alaska big-game hunting to troops.

Governor Sarah Palin today informed Alaska National Guardsmen and women serving in combat that big-game hunting opportunities will be available when they return from combat zones this fall.

"I heard from many Alaskans serving overseas during my trip to Kuwait in July," said Governor Palin. "One of the most frequent questions was about the status of hunting seasons upon their return. While I can't grant our troops the chance to hunt in closed areas or in places with species restrictions, I do want to recognize them and help them hunt this late fall or winter when they get home."

The Alaska Department of Fish and Game will reissue permits for service members who were successful in obtaining lottery permit hunts but were unable to use them. Service members are encouraged to contact their local ADF&G office to learn more about the hunting opportunities that may be available to them.

Source: Alaska Governor's Office: press release, "National Guardsmen," September 6, 2007.

Obligation to support our troops.

Operation America Rising is a newly founded, non-partisan organization whose sole mission is to show the men and women of the United States Armed Forces that they are supported. It is because of our fighting men and women that we are able to know freedom

While many will criticize the merits of war, we must all understand our obligation to support our fellow citizens who are putting their lives on the line to guarantee our freedoms for future generations.

Americans realize they can never fully repay our troops for the sacrifices they have made. These heroes face long deployments that separate them from their family and friends.

On July 7th in every state of our nation, Americans will gather together to express their deep appreciation for our troops. We owe it to the men and women of our armed forces. They deserve to know that they are supported by their fellow Americans.

Source: Alaska Governor's Office: Proclamation, "America Rising," June 27, 2007.

Proclaim "Loyalty Day" to reaffirm loyalty to America.

"Loyalty Day is a special day for the reaffirmation of loyalty to the US and for the recognition of the heritage of American freedom. Throughout our history, honorable men and women have demonstrated their loyalty to America by making remarkable sacrifices to preserve and protect these values.

"All Americans can be confident in the future of our nation as these values are passed on to each new generation. Our children need to know that our nation is a force for good in the world and must understand our past as they prepare to lead in the future.

"Each of us should celebrate the gift of freedom that has been earned for us by loyal Americans and join their efforts to ensure that our nation is kept strong so we can continue to live as free people."

NOW, THEREFORE, I Governor Sarah Palin, do hereby proclaim May 1, 2007 as Loyalty Day in Alaska, and call upon Alaskans to join in and support this national observance, display the flag of the United States, and reaffirm our allegiance to our nation.

Source: Alaska Governor's Office: Proclamation, "Loyalty Day." April 27, 2007.

Promote from within, in Alaska's National Guard.

"Thank you military personnel! I support you. I respect our military personnel and understand the importance of Alaska's National Guard. As I watched our military men and women being deployed I recognized how important it is for their families to know how much Alaska and America support them. I believe in 'promoting from within' to provide continued good leadership that truly understands Alaska and will partner with our elected leaders to support our troops."

Source: Campaign website, www.palinforgovernor.com, "Issues," November 7, 2006.

JOBS

Alaska Construction Academy.

We have some great news to share about a successful partnership involving the Alaska Department of Labor and Workforce Development. This venture produced the Alaska Construction Academy, and now, more than 2,300 middle and high school students and 320 adults are learning new skills—such as carpentry, plumbing, electrical, welding, and drywall finishing. The academy started as a pilot program in Anchorage to attract and train young people and adults to find jobs in the Alaska construction industry.

This program has been so successful, more will follow elsewhere statewide. Graduates will help fill the 1,000 construction jobs that are needed annually.

Out of the first group of 113 Anchorage adult graduates, 77 percent were hired and increased their earnings 40 percent in the two quarters following their training. Adult classes are offered at various times, based on community employer needs, and will be expanded to include weatherization programs.

Source: Alaska Governor's Office: August 2008 Newsletter, August 20, 2008.

Leverage job-training dollars through vocational and technical curriculum.

I will leverage job-training dollars through efficiencies in government, private-sector partnerships, and responsible investments in job-training opportunities that result in good jobs for Alaskans. I look forward to working with a cross section of citizen advisors who represent private-sector employers' educational institutions, union and non-union training programs, and other workforce development professionals on the Alaska Workforce Investment Board. With their advice, we can meet the rapidly growing need for trained workers. I am a strong proponent of a vocational and technical curriculum in our schools and will focus on this area to get our workforce ready for the future. I don't want to see an importation of Alaska's workforce when we have untapped talent here in the state, anxious for training and anxious for the opportunity to work.

Source: Palin-Parnell campaign booklet: *New Energy for Alaska,* November 3, 2006.

Focus Workforce Investment Board on vocational careers.

Workforce Readiness for Students: Alaska's youths have tremendous career opportunities in the skilled trades if they have adequate training. I will charge the Alaska Workforce Investment Board (AWIB) with drawing upon its considerable expertise to develop a pilot program aimed at increasing awareness of vocational career opportunities for our younger students through a partnership with industries facing worker shortages. The pilot will be industry-focused and include a streamlined and efficient administrative process to encourage industry participation. It will consider children's safety first and be designed with exciting field trips and industry-based learning activities.

Source: Palin-Parnell campaign booklet: *New Energy for Alaska,* November 3, 2006

Praised the Red Dog Zinc Mine for bringing rural jobs.

The major candidates for governor can't go anywhere in Alaska without discussing Pebble, the gigantic mineral, copper and gold deposit north of Iliamna. The following are the candidates' positions.

Knowles claims strong opposition. At a resource industry forum in Anchorage, Knowles said he finds the Pebble project "terrifying." Knowles said recently, "The scale of it is so enormous. On its merits, (Pebble) is an unacceptable risk."

Palin is reserving judgment on Pebble, for now. On the Pebble project, Palin says she would not put one resource, such as the Bristol Bay salmon fishery, at risk "for another resource."

In recent debates, Palin has rarely commented on individual mines, though she praised the Red Dog Zinc Mine near Kotzebue for bringing jobs to rural Alaska.

SUMMARY: TONY KNOWLES: Thinks the Pebble mine prospect is "terrifying."

SARAH PALIN: Withholding judgment until she sees Pebble permit applications, but unwilling to risk the region's fisheries.

Source: *Anchorage Daily News*: 2006 gubernatorial candidate profile, October 31, 2006.

Department of Fish and Game is underfunded.

Knowles and Palin, courting the fish crowd is *de rigueur*. More than 20,000 commercial fishermen chase fish. More than 200,000 residents hold sport-fishing licenses. And 83 percent of rural households have subsistence fishing permits.

All the candidates say the Alaska Department of Fish and Game is underfunded, lacking enough people and tools to study and protect the fish and their habitat.

All also promise to appoint people to the State Board of Fisheries and the North Pacific Council, who will put the health of fish stocks first and won't let politics interfere.

Knowles vows he won't appoint "lightning rods," but his commercial critics argue he did as governor, naming people with sport-fishing or environmental bents such as Kenai River sport fishing kingpin Bob Penney.

"What I was trying to do was bring a real balance," Knowles said. Indeed, the makeup of the board and council have at times tilted heavily toward commercial fishing interests.

Source: *Anchorage Daily News*: 2006 gubernatorial candidate profile, October 29, 2006.

Unions should get member permission for political donations.

Q: Do you support legislation requiring labor unions to obtain permission from their members before using dues for political purposes?

A: Yes, unions represent their workers and, as such, should be accountable to them

Source: Eagle Forum 2006 Gubernatorial Candidate Questionnaire, July 31, 2006.

PRINCIPLES AND VALUES

Small-town values.

"Long ago, a young farmer and haberdasher from Missouri followed an unlikely path to the vice presidency. A writer observed: 'We grow good people in our small towns, with honesty, sincerity, and dignity.' I know just the kind of people that writer had in mind when he praised Harry Truman. I grew up with those people. They do some of the hardest work in America— those who grow our food, run our factories, and fight our wars. They love their country, in good times and bad, and they're always proud of America."

Source: Speech at 2008 Republican National Convention, September 3, 2008.

Denies all allegations in Department of Public Safety affair.

Governor Sarah Palin today released the following statement regarding allegations that she acted improperly:

"To allege that I, or any member of my family, requested, received, or released confidential personnel information on an Alaska State Trooper, or directed disciplinary action be taken against any employee of the Department of Public Safety, is, quite simply, outrageous. Any information regarding personnel records came from the trooper himself. I question the timing of these false allegations. It is unfortunate, as we seek to address a growing energy crisis in this state, that this matter has been raised now.

"I do not interfere with the day-to-day operations of any department. I have and will continue to support our line troopers. They have my utmost respect. Since taking office, I have proposed to the legislature millions of dollars in budget increases for more troopers, equipment and training."

Source: Alaska Governor's Office: press release, "Acting improperly," July 17, 2008.

Declared a National Day of Prayer in Alaska.

• WHEREAS, the Continental Congress called for a National Day of Prayer in 1775. In 1863, President Lincoln established a proclamation for a day of "humiliation, fasting, and prayer." And in 1988, President Reagan set aside the first Thursday in May as the National Day of Prayer.

• WHEREAS, following the devastating event on Sept. 11, 2001, President Bush called on citizens to reaffirm the role of prayer in our society and to honor the religious diversity our freedom permits by recognizing this day annually.

• WHEREAS, it is not the intent of this proclamation to promote a particular religion, but rather to encourage thoughtful reflection and to honor our freedom of religious expression whether that is prayer, meditation, peace activism, or another form of contemplative action.

• NOW, THEREFORE, I, Governor Sarah Palin, do hereby proclaim May 1, 2008, as National Day of Prayer in Alaska and encourage Alaskans to keep the health, prosperity, and peace of our state, nation, and world in mind on this day.

Source: Alaska Governor's Office: Proclamation, "Day of Prayer," April 15, 2008.

Leadership has a responsibility to prepare for tomorrow.

"We are on the same team, if we have the same goal. With so much opportunity in Alaska, let's look at challenges like we do in our own families: save money, spend wisely, and we will secure our tomorrow. Invest in solid foundations, like education and deferred maintenance. Pull together, not tear down. Be positive. Respect our treasured past, but look forward now. These are leadership characteristics expected by those who elect us to lead, to serve, and to work for Alaskans. What a responsibility we have! To look beyond partisan and geographic differences. To slow government growth, so we don't tax hard-working families and hand future generations a budget they can't afford. To restore trust in government. To develop our resources responsibly, including a gas line to meet our long-term energy needs. To equip our students for work and help them commit to personal responsibility and good character. United leadership to do the will of the people, with vigor."

Source: State of the State Address to the 25th Alaska Legislature, January 15, 2008.

The Bible has profoundly influenced America.

• WHEREAS, since the earliest days of our democracy, Americans have turned to the Bible for divine guidance, comfort, and encouragement.

• WHEREAS, the Bible has profoundly influenced art, literature, music, and codes of law.

• WHEREAS, the Bible has motivated many to acts of compassion, humanity, and charity.

• WHEREAS, the Bible continues to provide motivation, inspiration, hope, and comfort for countless Alaskans.

• WHEREAS, the National Bible Association reminds Alaskans and people of all faiths of the Bible's unique place in American life.

• NOW, THEREFORE, I, Sarah Palin, Governor of the State of Alaska, do hereby proclaim November 18-25, 2007, as Bible Week in Alaska, and encourage interested citizens to participate in this observance.

Source: Alaska Governor's Office: Press release, "Bible Week," October 17, 2007.

Recognize America's historic and founding Christian heritage.

• WHEREAS, the celebration of Christian Heritage Week reminds Alaskans of the role Christianity has played in our rich heritage. Many truly great men and women of America, giants in the structuring of American history, were Christians of caliber and integrity who did not hesitate to express their faith:

• WHEREAS, the Preamble to the Constitution of the State of Alaska begins with, "We the people of Alaska, grateful to God and to those who founded our nation...."

• WHEREAS, George Washington enunciated, "Animated alone by the pure spirit of Christianity ... we may enjoy every temporal and spiritual felicity."

• WHEREAS, James Madison, father of the United States Constitution, advocated, "The diffusion of the light of Christianity in our nation" in his Memorial and Remonstrance.

• NOW, THEREFORE, I, Governor Sarah Palin, do hereby proclaim October 21-27, 2007, as Alaska's 9th Annual Christian Heritage Week in Alaska, and encourage all citizens to celebrate this week.

Source: Alaska Governor's Office: Proclamation, "Christian Heritage." September 14, 2007.

Top priorities for Alaska include ethics and a balanced budget.

"One hundred days ago, I outlined my top priorities for the state: a natural-gas line, a balanced budget including temporary relief for the unexpected PERS/ TRS (Public Employees' and Teachers' Retirement System) burden, ethics reform, and workforce development," said Governor Palin. "I am proud of our accomplishments to date, but we still have a lot of work to do."

Source: Alaska Governor's Office: press release, "100th Day," March 13, 2007.

Decries "politics as usual."

Knowles rallied in the third round when talk turned to Palin's habit of skipping campaign events. Though Palin tried to move the conversation in another direction, decrying the topic as "politics as usual," she derailed her effort by engaging in a politics-as-usual debate over the definition of the phrase "no-show." The moderator cut them off to end the silliness.

Source: Alaska 2006 Governor Debate: ADN coverage of radio debate, November 3, 2006.

Fight for freedom of religion and freedom of expression.

Q: How would you feel if you walked into a church and heard a pastor endorse a candidate for governor?

KNOWLES: Freedom of speech. I don't mind what is said from the pulpit.

PALIN: A pastor, a priest, a rabbi, certainly they have the freedom to say whatever they want to say. And you know, thank the Lord that we do have that freedom of speech. Faith is very important to so many of us here in America, and I would never support any government effort to stifle our freedom of religion or freedom of expression or freedom of speech. I would just caution a pastor to be very careful if they're in front of a congregation and they decide to endorse one candidate over another. There may be some frustration with that candidacy endorsement being made manifest by fewer dollars in the offering plate. But, no, I'll tell you, freedom of speech is so precious and it's worth defending and of course freedom of religion and freedom of expression will be things that I will fight for.

Source: Alaska 2006 Governor Debate: KAKM-7 with Michael Carey, October 25, 2006.

SOCIAL SECURITY

Fund the Seniors Longevity Bonus Program. Home-based assistance is more cost-effective than institutions.

I support funding our Seniors Longevity Bonus Program, so the program can phase out on schedule in agreement with public discussion years ago. The program was declining and it was a shame to see our esteemed pioneers face broken promises when they were prematurely lopped off the program. I also support home and community based assistance programs, which are more cost effective than institutional alternatives and also allow seniors to stay in their homes and communities with dignity. Senior citizens will be respected in my administration and will receive our full respect and support. They are my delight and I will not let them down.

Source: Palin-Parnell campaign booklet: *New Energy for Alaska,* November 3, 2006.

TAX REFORM

Raising taxes hurts small businesses and jobs.

"The Democratic nominee for president supports plans to raise income taxes ... raise payroll taxes ... raise investment income taxes ... raise the death tax ... raise business taxes ... and increase the tax burden on the American people by hundreds of billions of dollars.

My sister Heather and her husband have just built a service station that's now opened for business—like millions of others who run small businesses. How are they going to be any better off if taxes go up?

Or maybe you're trying to keep your job at a plant in Michigan or Ohio ... or create jobs with clean coal from Pennsylvania or West Virginia ... or keep a small farm in the family right here in Minnesota. How are you going to be better off if our opponent adds a massive tax burden to the American economy?"

Source: Speech at 2008 Republican National Convention, September 3, 2008.

Cut taxes.

Palin was just 28 when her political star began its rapid ascent. Urged on by city activists, she ran for and won a seat on the Wasilla City Council, in part to help promote economic development in the small valley town.

Four years later, she was elected as Wasilla's mayor, knocking off three-term incumbent John Stein by promising tax cuts, spending reform, and a fresh face leading the city. Palin largely delivered on her promises.

Source: *Boston Globe*, "A Valentine to Evangelical Base," p. A12, August 30, 2008.

Allotted $60 million annually for municipal revenue sharing.

Governor Sarah Palin today thanked legislators for their efforts in passing Senate Bill 72. SB 72, pertaining to municipal revenue sharing, sets up a structure for distributing $60 million each year to local governments for the next three years.

"As a former mayor and city council member, it is my belief that services are best provided at the most local level possible," Governor Palin said. "I am pleased that Senate members have committed to fund municipal revenue sharing for the next three years. They took our proposal and made it better, and I appreciate them for working together to accomplish this."

Under municipal revenue sharing, the state distributes funds to the municipalities of Alaska. The local entities have discretionary use of the funds, which can be used for a variety of purposes, such as providing larger communities the ability to offer tax relief to its residents and providing smaller communities with funds to help support basic municipal services.

Source: Governor's office press release, "Senate Bill 72," March 12, 2008.

Eliminate taxes that inhibit business.

"I will propose reducing or eliminating burdensome taxes on our citizens, like business license fees and the tire tax. After our citizens, our state treasure is our commonly owned natural resources. Fifty years ago, our constitution's founders established lofty goals and ironclad promises to be self-sufficient and self-determined in our wise use of resources."

Source: State of the State Address to the 25th Alaska Legislature, January 15, 2008.

Repeal "nuisance taxes."

"To help Alaska's families, and small businesses (the backbone of our local economies), I propose to repeal "nuisance taxes" including the tire tax—we shouldn't make Alaskans pay a premium to keep families safe while driving Alaska's roads. And we'll significantly reduce business license fees and taxes, which send the wrong message by financially discouraging our small businesses."

Source: State of the State Address to the 24th Alaska Legislature, January 17, 2007.

Mitigate impact of new $50-million annual cruise-ship tourism tax.

Thirteen days after the next governor takes the oath of office, Alaska will enact sweeping new rules and taxes on the tourism industry. Just a few months ago, Alaska voters put cruise lines and their passengers on the hook for millions in new taxes and fees, all contained in a cruise-ship ballot proposition approved in August's primary election.

Sarah Palin now says she doesn't feel comfortable with some aspects of the new law. She recently told tourism industry officials that if elected, she would work with them to "mitigate some of the impacts" of the law.

The new taxes and fees will generate at least $50 million a year in additional state revenue, according to recent estimates from the Alaska Department of Revenue. For the first time, the state also will put observers on cruise ships visiting Alaska to monitor the ships' smokestack and waste-water emissions. And cruise lines will need to begin disclosing their sales commissions with on-shore vendors.

Source: *Anchorage Daily News*: 2006 gubernatorial candidate profile, October 30, 2006.

No income tax.

Q: If the state finds itself squeezed for funds in the future, where would you look for more revenue?

A: Unlike my opponents' efforts in the past, I will not propose to take the people's dividends or impose an income tax. Given our current revenue projections, I will focus my administration toward developing our natural resources and establishing an agreement to build a gas pipeline.

Q: Should the state consider using more Permanent Fund earnings to run government?

A: No.

Source: *Anchorage Daily News*: 2006 gubernatorial candidate profile, October 22, 2006.

Supports a seasonal sales tax.

Q: Would you support state sales or income taxes under any circumstances?

A: I don't support state income taxes. There are circumstances where I could support a sales tax, if applied seasonally.

Q: Are there sectors of the Alaska economy that are under-taxed or over-taxed? Which ones?

A: As a fiscal conservative, I'm not enamored with additional taxes on anything. I believe it's the governor's job to make sure the state gets a fair return on the development of our natural resources.

Source: *Anchorage Daily News*: 2006 gubernatorial candidate profile, October 22, 2006.

TECHNOLOGY

Supports $130 million in research investment in University of Alaska.

Research is a huge part of how a university can help pay its own way. The University of Alaska is currently leveraging federal dollars for research to the tune of $1 in state funds for every $7 in federal funds. The $130 million received annually in research dollars is an investment in our students and our University of Alaska system.

Source: Palin-Parnell campaign booklet: *New Energy for Alaska,* November 3, 2006.

Efficient transportation system is vital.

An efficient and functional transportation system is absolutely vital to our economy. Throughout history, strong transportation systems have been the cornerstone of economic growth and success throughout the world. It is equally important in Alaska, where so much of our state is remote and still not connected by roads. Transportation infrastructure is a basic necessity that Alaska must have to succeed and prosper. Improvement and expansion to our aging network of public facilities, roads, harbors, airports, and railways is required for any development, and gas-line construction success. A highly functional, well-maintained, statewide transportation network of public facilities, roads, ferries, trains, and airports is required to improve Alaska's economy and the quality of life for ALL Alaskans.

Source: Palin-Parnell campaign booklet: *New Energy for Alaska*, November 3, 2006.

Supports a state-funded highway program.

It is time for Alaska to develop a state-funded highway program like most states in America. This will be a challenge for us, but it is necessary to reduce our current near total dependency on federal aid and ensure basic needs and maintenance are addressed.

• Our Marine Highway is a critical service covering the largest area of any state coastline in America.

• Alaska ferries are essential to link and connect our island and coastal communities to the rest of Alaska, Canada, and the lower 48.

Source: Palin-Parnell campaign booklet: *New Energy for Alaska*, November 3, 2006.

CHAPTER 7

The Big Reveal

Before the speeches were given, the transcripts were released to the media. This historical time in Sarah Palin's life took place at the 2008 Republican National Convention. I share it in this book because it so clearly lets you see who she is; it reveals her transparency, sincerity, and intellect. The whole world listened as Senator John McCain began his announcement:

> I'm very happy—I'm very happy today to spend my birthday with you and to make a historic announcement in Dayton, a city built on hard, honest work of good people.
>
> Like the entire industrial Midwest, Dayton has contributed much to the prosperity and progress of America, and now, in these tough, changing times, after all you've done for our country, you want your government to understand what you're going through, to stand on your side, and fight for you.

And that's what I intend to do.

That's why I'm running for president: to fight for you, to make government stand on your side, not in your way.

Friends, I've spent the last few months looking for a running mate who can best help me shake up Washington and make it start working again for the people that are counting on us.

As I'm sure you know, I had many good people to choose from, all of them dedicated to this country and to getting us back on the road to prosperity and peace. And I am very grateful to all of them, and honored by their willingness to serve with me.

And I'm going to continue to rely on their support and counsel during this campaign, and after we win this election, when the real work begins.

But I could only choose one. And it's with great pride and gratitude that I tell you I have found the right partner to help me stand up to those who value their privileges over their responsibilities, who put power over principle, and put their interests before your needs.

I found someone with an outstanding reputation for standing up to special interests and entrenched bureaucracies; someone who has fought against corruption and the failed policies of the past; someone who's stopped government from wasting taxpayers' money...on things they don't want or need and put it back to work for the people; someone with executive experience, who has shown great tenacity and skill in tackling tough problems, especially our dangerous dependence on foreign oil; someone who reached across the aisle and asked Republicans, Democrats and independents to serve in government; someone with strong principles of a fighting spirit and deep compassion ... someone who grew up in a decent, hard-working, middle-class family, whose father was an elementary school teacher and whose mother was the school secretary.

They taught their children to care about others, to work hard and to stand up with courage for the things you believe in.

Both of them were coaches, too, and raised their children to excel at sports.

And I'm sure they taught them skills that will surely come in handy over the next two months.

The person I'm about to introduce to you was a union member and is married to a union member and understands the problems, the hopes and the values of working people, knows what it's like to worry about mortgage payments and health care and the cost of gasoline and groceries; a standout high school point guard; a concerned citizen who became a member of the PTA, then a city council member, and then a mayor, and now a governor ... who beat the long odds to win a tough election on a message of reform and public integrity. And I am especially proud to say in the week we celebrate the anniversary of women's suffrage, a devoted wife and a mother of five.

She's not—she's not from these parts and she's not from Washington. But when you get to know her, you're going to be as impressed as I am.

She's got the grit, integrity, and good sense and fierce devotion to the common good that is exactly what we need in Washington today.

She knows where she comes from, and she knows who she works for. She stands up for what's right, and she doesn't let anyone tell her to sit down.

She's fought oil companies and party bosses and do-nothing bureaucrats and anyone who puts their interests before the interests of the people she swore an oath to serve.

She's exactly who I need. She's exactly who this country needs to help me fight ... to help me fight the same old Washington politics of me first and country second.

My friends and fellow Americans ... I am very pleased and very privileged to introduce to you the next Vice-president of the United States ... Governor Sarah Palin of the great State of Alaska.

Sarah Palin greeted the crowd and spoke these words:

Thank you so much.

And I thank you, Senator McCain and Mrs. McCain, for the confidence that you have placed in me. Senator, I am honored to be chosen as your running mate.

I will be honored to serve next to the next President of the United States.

I know that when Senator McCain gave me this opportunity, he had a short list of highly qualified men and women. And to have made that list at all, it was a privilege. And to have been chosen brings a great challenge.

I know that it will demand the best that I have to give, and I promise nothing less.

First—first, there are a few people whom I would like you to meet. I want to start with my husband, Todd.

And Todd and I are actually celebrating our 20th anniversary today. And I promised him...

I had promised Todd a little surprise for the anniversary present, and hopefully he knows that I did deliver.

And then we have as—after my husband, who is a lifelong commercial fisherman, lifetime Alaskan. He's a production operator.

Todd is a production operator in the oil fields up on Alaska's North Slope. And he's a proud

★ 127 ★

SARAH PALIN: Faith—Family—Country

member of the United Steelworkers union. And he's a world-champion snow machine racer.

Todd and I met way back in high school. And I can tell you that he is still the man that I admire most in this world.

Along the way, Todd and I have shared many blessings. And four out of five of them are here with us today.

Our oldest son, Track, though, he'll be following the presidential campaign from afar. On September 11th of last year, our son enlisted in the United States Army.

Track now serves in an infantry brigade. And on September 11th, Track will deploy to Iraq in the service of his country. And Todd and I are so proud of him and of all the fine men and women serving this country.

Next to Todd is our daughter, Bristol, another daughter, Willow, our youngest daughter, Piper, and over in their arms is our son, Trig, a beautiful baby boy. He was born just in April.

His name is Trig Paxson Van Palin.

Some of life's greatest opportunities come unexpectedly. And this is certainly the case today.

I never really set out to be involved in public affairs, much less to run for this office. My mom and dad both worked at the local elementary school. And my husband and I, we both grew up working with our hands. I was just your average hockey mom in Alaska.

We're busy raising our kids. I was serving as the team mom and coaching some basketball on the side. I got involved in the PTA and then was elected to the city council, and then elected mayor of my hometown, where my agenda was to stop wasteful spending, and cut property taxes, and put the people first.

I was then appointed ethics commissioner and Chairman of the Alaska Oil and Gas Conservation Commission. And when I found corruption there, I fought it hard, and I held the offenders to account.

Along with fellow reformers in the great State of Alaska, as governor, I've stood up to the old politics as usual, to the special interests, to the lobbyists, the big oil companies, and the good-old-boy network.

When oil and gas prices went up so dramatically and the state revenues followed with that increase, I sent a large share of that revenue directly back to the people of Alaska. And we are now—we're now embarking on a $40 billion natural-gas pipeline to help lead America to energy independence.

I signed major ethics reform. And I appointed both Democrats and independents to serve in my administration. And I championed reform to end the abuses of earmark spending by congress.

In fact, I told congress, "Thanks, but no thanks," on that bridge to nowhere.

If our state wanted a bridge, I said we'd build it ourselves. Well, it's always, though, safer in politics to avoid risk, to just kind of go along with the status quo. But I didn't get into government to do the safe and easy things. A ship in harbor is safe, but that's not why the ship is built.

Politics isn't just a game of competing interests and clashing parties. The people of America expect us to seek public office and to serve for the right reasons.

And the right reason is to challenge the status quo and to serve the common good.

Now, no one expects us to agree on everything, whether in Juneau or in Washington. But we are expected to govern with integrity, and goodwill, and clear convictions, and a servant's heart.

Now, no leader in America has shown these qualities so clearly or presents so clear a threat to business as usual in Washington as Senator John S. McCain.

This is a moment when principles and political independence matter a lot more than just the party line. And this is a man who has always been there to serve his country, not just his party.

And this is a moment that requires resolve and toughness, and strength of heart in the American president. And my running mate is a man who has shown those qualities in the darkest of places, and in the service of his country.

A colleague once said about Senator McCain, "That man did things for this country that few people could go through. Never forget that." And that speaker was former Senator John Glenn of Ohio.

And John Glenn knows something about heroism. And I'm going to make sure nobody does forget that in this campaign. There is only one candidate who has truly fought for America, and that man is John McCain.

This is a moment—this is a moment when great causes can be won and great threats overcome, depending on the judgment of our next president.

In a dangerous world, it is John McCain who will lead America's friends and allies in preventing Iran from acquiring nuclear weapons.

It was John McCain who cautioned long ago about the harm that Russian aggression could do to Georgia and to other small democratic neighbors and to the world oil markets.

It was Senator McCain who refused to hedge his support for our troops in Iraq, regardless of the political costs.

And you know what? As the mother of one of those troops, and as the commander of Alaska's National Guard, that's the kind of man I want as our commander-in-chief.

Profiles in courage: They can be hard to come by these days. You know, so often we just find them in books. But next week when we nominate John McCain for president, we're putting one on the ballot.

To serve as vice president beside such a man would be the privilege of a lifetime. And it's fitting that this trust has been given to me 88 years almost to the day after the women of America first gained the right to vote.

I think as well today of two other women who came before me in national elections. I can't begin this great effort without honoring the achievements of Geraldine Ferraro in 1984, and of course Senator Hillary Clinton, who showed such determination and grace in her presidential campaign.

It was rightly noted in Denver this week that Hillary left 18 million cracks in the highest, hardest glass ceiling in America ... but it turns out the women of America aren't finished yet and we can shatter that glass ceiling once and for all.

So for my part, the mission is clear: The next 67 days I'm going to take our campaign to every part of our country and our message of reform to every voter of every background in every political party, or no party at all.

If you want change in Washington, if you hope for a better America, then we're asking for your vote on the 4th of November.

My fellow Americans, come join our cause.

Join our cause and help our country to elect a great man as the next President of the United States.

And I thank you, and God bless you; I say, and God bless America. Thank you.

Sources

All sources for information in this biography have provided permission for their use.

Chapter 6: Copyright 2008, The Speakout Foundation and OnTheIssues.org, Jesse Gordon, editor-in-chief. Used by permission.

http://www.cityofwasilla.com/

http://gov.state.ak.us/

Wikipedia: http://en.wikipedia.org/wiki/Sarah_palin

http://rncnyc2004.blogspot.com/2008/08/governor-sarah-palin-biography.html

www.johnmccain.com/

Used with permission: Frank Wallis, Baxter Bulletin, September 10, 2008.

http://www.baxterbulletin.com/apps/pbcs.dll/article?AID=/200809100500/NEWS01/809100326

Sally Heath, 2008.

Chuck Heath, 2008.

Mary Ellan Moe, 2008.

Karena Forster and Ben Harrell Used with permission, 2008.

Ruth Andree, 2008.

Photos used with permission of Ruth Andree, 2008.

Deanna Andree, 2008.

http://www.johnmccain.com/about/governorpalin. htm?sid=googleandt=palin

Wikipedia: http://en.wikipedia.org/wiki/Sarah_palin

Copyright 2008 The Speakout Foundation and OnTheIssues. org, Jesse Gordon, Editor-in-Chief. Used with permission.

Anchorage Daily News: 2006 gubernatorial candidate profile, October 22, 2006.

Anchorage Daily News: "Little play," by K. Hopkins, August 6, 2006.

Palin-Parnell campaign booklet: *New Energy for Alaska,* November 3, 2006.

Anchorage Daily News: 2006 gubernatorial candidate profile, October 30, 2006.

Anchorage Daily News: "Little play," by K. Hopkins, August 6, 2006.

Anchorage Daily News: 2006 gubernatorial candidate profile, October 22, 2006.

Anchorage Daily News: 2006 gubernatorial candidate profile, October 30, 2006.